T0346341

# THE PLIGHT OF POTENTIAL

# THE PLIGHT OF POTENTIAL

## EMBRACING SOLITUDE IN MILLENNIAL LIFE AND MODERN WORK

EMERSON CSORBA

ANTHEM PRESS

Anthem Press
An imprint of Wimbledon Publishing Company
*www.anthempress.com*

This edition first published in UK and USA 2018
by ANTHEM PRESS
75–76 Blackfriars Road, London SE1 8HA, UK
or PO Box 9779, London SW19 7ZG, UK
and
244 Madison Ave #116, New York, NY 10016, USA

*British Library Cataloguing-in-Publication Data*
A catalogue record for this book is available from the British Library.

ISBN-13: 978-1-78308-657-3 (Hbk)
ISBN-10: 1-78308-657-2 (Hbk)

This title is also available as an e-book.

# CONTENTS

# ACKNOWLEDGMENTS

Albert Bandura wrote in 1982 about the psychology of chance encounters, stating that some of the most important determinants of our lives arise from the most unexpected of circumstances. This book is no exception. I have been fortunate to meet a wide variety of thinkers over the past years—many unexpectedly—who have provided no shortage of ideas upon which to reflect.

Marc Arnal, from the University of Alberta's Campus Saint-Jean, the university's Francophone college, spurred much of this initial intellectual exploration, in addition to a formative English professor Dalbir Sehmby. Don Carmichael later instilled in me an appreciation for philosophy that has provided grounding for much of my intellectual journey thus far. At the University of Cambridge, Ian Frowe pushed me to think about where *I* stood on a range of philosophical and educational issues, thus contributing significantly to much of the thinking that has gone into this book.

In business, the opportunity to run Gen Y Inc. at the beginning of my career profoundly shaped my view of the world, particularly in terms of developing patience and skepticism in the creation of new business engagements. The projects of which Gen Y Inc. was a part provided the initial impetus to write this book. I'm grateful to each person who has made this work possible, whether former partners (Eric Termuende) or our early clients (Tom Thompson, Chris Lumb and Landon Leclair are deserving of particular thanks). Simona Chiose provided opportunities to reflect on these experiences through the written word, which in hindsight were transformative. I thank her for her generosity. As I entered the next stage of business endeavors, Noa Gafni has been a wonderful partner, our projects having a major impact on my life, particularly in relation to reflection on faith-based communities. Similarly, the projects and conversations with Cameron Raynor, Kanishka Narayan, Kalm Paul-Christian, Fin O'Kane, Ellen Quigley and Paul de Sciscio, whether in Canada or the United Kingdom, have provided copious material for personal reflection.

Several individuals deserve particular thanks in the writing of this book. Catrin Owen provided the necessary encouragement to put the book concept into full motion. Without her, the project would have never begun. Sameer Dhar is the best friend that a person could ever ask for, and is a constant reminder of what it means to live with purpose, integrity and care for the most vulnerable. He is a role model to his friends on both sides of the Atlantic.

Eric Newell, one of the great builders of his generation, has provided unwavering support over past years, doing so with utmost humility. He is a source of continual wisdom in terms of what it means to live a good life. Finally, I'm grateful to Tom Hunt, Max Harris and Logan Graham for their collective encouragement and penetrating comments in the early stages of writing. I have greatly enjoyed the wit and sense of humor of Tom, an accomplished writer himself, in our many conversations. Max's own experiences writing a successful first book, and his deep knowledge of politics and philosophy, have similarly given me much food for thought over the last year. And Logan, whose curiosity and intellect are daunting, to say the least, has provided many opportunities for reflection and laughter throughout this project.

Anthem Press has been a patient and understanding partner over the course of this book's development. Tej Sood, in particular, has been consistently attentive and committed throughout this process, and I look forward to working together in the next stages of this project. At the University of Oxford, my thanks go to Nigel Biggar for his thoughtfulness in the final stages of writing.

And of course, the deepest gratitude to my mum, Marla Csorba, for her constant reminders to progress in the writing despite the other projects that have consumed my attention, for better or worse, over the past two years. This book is dedicated to you.

I now eagerly await the many conversations that I can only hope this book will spur. Of course, any errors in this book are mine alone.

# INTRODUCTION

What do we mean when we talk about our *potential*? Modern life involves a lot of thinking about this idea. There is a big focus on pursuing self-growth, on dreaming big and doing whatever we can to achieve the visions we've set for ourselves. We believe that people are unique and special in their talents and that we must celebrate this. What each person's potential *is*, exactly, might be unclear, and yet constant striving for self-betterment consumes the thinking of those living in the modern era.

Modern life demands this kind of thinking, and we've come to take it for granted. Not surprisingly, few people question the notion of potential: who, after all, does *not* want to grow, or *not* take advantage of their gifts and talents? Who does not want to see themselves as being limitless in their capacity for achievement? And so an important part of life becomes a matter of consistently working to achieve our individual potentialities, though often with little reflection on what our respective journeys are really for.

In his book *Missing Out: In Praise of the Unlived Life*, the British psychoanalyst Adam Phillips writes, "The myth of our potential can make of our lives a perpetual falling-short, a continual and continuing loss […] though at its best it lures us into the future, but without letting us wonder why such lures are required."[1] There is an allure to our belief in potential, allowing individuals to live in what *could be*, rather than in what is. The person in pursuit of potential is in a constant state of self-discovery, and so can be excused for being restless, never really slowing down or making serious decisions as to what they want to do in life.

As Phillips suggests, it is possible—perhaps likely, even—that our wished-for lives, centered on this belief in potential, limit self-examination in important ways. To dedicate time and space for critical self-examination in the present is hard work. This involves the confrontation of self, which can be slow, frustrating and painful, but there is little need for this kind of inner dialogue when the modern world always points us toward the future. In modern life we tend to associate potential with variety: we unlock our potential by doing as many things as possible in the shortest amount of time. Through variety, it is possible to sample from our many imagined lives. This keeps doors open to interesting future opportunities in life and work.

For those currently coming of age—that is, the "millennial" generation— a myriad of factors encourage this emphasis on potential. These are worth a very brief overview. Sherry Turkle, who serves as the Abby Rockefeller Mauzé Professor of the Social Studies of Science and Technology at the Massachusetts Institute of Technology (MIT), offers insight into one of these pressures: that of networks. In her book *Alone Together*, Turkle writes that "the network is seductive […] if we are always on, we may deny ourselves the rewards of solitude."[2] Networks offer the promise of efficiency—providing individuals with opportunities to connect with large volumes of people in little time—though often these very technologies consume users.

Another factor is that of societal change. Narratives about perpetual change and uncertainty—specifically, of a "rapidly changing world"—abound, which heighten individual anxiety and contribute to considerable worry regarding how best to live in this kind of world. At the same time, perpetual change and uncertainty bring new opportunities, from which the most active and flexible individuals can supposedly benefit.

A third pressure relates to educational institutions, particularly universities. In universities, the word of the day is now "adaptability." Chief among universities' priorities is to ensure that students graduate with the ability to adapt themselves to a wide variety of work and life circumstances, which are considered unpredictable. On the surface, this might seem benign—why *not* help students develop the dispositions to transition easily from one type of work to another? This point seems obvious. So universities encourage the ability to sell and take action (rather than to inform oneself and ask questions) in order to help graduates transition seamlessly into whatever the world puts in their way.

This book is about millennials, work and solitude. It is about those currently coming of age, in the early stages of their careers and actively thinking about the kinds of lives that they want to lead. This book is in large part a critique of things that we take for granted in modern life and that I believe harm us in ways that we do not usually see. The idea that we are limitless beings, destined to fulfill our potential, is one of these. In particular, I argue that millennials suffer—though not necessarily because of their own wrongdoing—from an inability to think critically about what kinds of lives they *really* want to lead, as *individuals*.

I must be careful about what I mean by *individuals*. We live in a society that at first glance values individualism, but that upon further inspection seems to frown upon people who actually take ownership in their own thinking. The individualism to which I refer is one where a person takes into consideration what others say and do, reflects and then makes sense of this in their own terms. This person is embedded in social structure and yet demonstrates autonomy in thinking and action within this structure—sometimes shaping the structure itself through this activity.

Despite the emphasis that we collectively place on ideas like potential (or perhaps *because* of such emphasis!), most of us glide from one activity to the next without much coherence or reflection. Generally, we seem lost in a world of possibilities, lacking the moral vocabulary required to think effectively about what it means to live a good life. Solitude plays a major role in the cultivation of the kind of inner life that I favor, but is difficult to practice in a world that is believed to move quickly, where those not working toward something measurable risk falling behind.

My sense, in observing friends and colleagues over past years, is that they are peripherally aware of the dangers in thinking about how they can always move forward, progress, advance, self-actualize or find their purpose (to name a few terms that we commonly hear), and yet aren't quite sure how to think independently about what kind of life is really worth leading *for them*.

My aim in this book is *not* to describe this generation, for this is ultimately a futile endeavor. A lot of writing has been published in newspapers and magazines about millennials, the majority of which is not very insightful. For almost three years, I led a company focused on intergenerational engagement and through this quickly came to realize that, despite the public interest in the topic, it is much better to speak about the *conditions* that shape the world in which millennials live than to make specific recommendations on how companies should treat members of this cohort in their workforces. This approach requires that we make some generalizations, which pertain mostly to the philosophical, economic and cultural contours that shape people's entry into adulthood.

I'm much more comfortable writing about broad conditions that I believe affect individual behavior in important ways than I am making any sweeping statements about a generational cohort. This approach, I think, implies that individuals will be affected by these conditions to varying degrees—some more, some less—and so provides necessary emphasis on individual freedom and autonomy. That said, I also do not want to shy away from making value judgments about modern life, for fear of offending individuals in our relativistic culture. My sense is that a great number of millennials feel lost precisely because they do not know how to make sense of the complicated world they inhabit.

More importantly, there is considerable hesitance to engage critically and respectfully with each other about what living a *good* life entails.

My efforts in this book are directed not toward telling readers what they should know about this cohort per se, nor what solutions can best engage this generation. I attempt instead to outline some major challenges that many of us face as we think about what kinds of lives are worth leading, given the pressures that make life seem like an endless search—and thus bring confusion and stress—for this generation. When I use the word "millennials," I'm referring to individuals generally in their twenties and thirties who are thinking actively, and making decisions, about what kinds of lives they really want to have.

Put differently, we can look at my intention this way: the term millennial is useful as a construct that reflects social, cultural, and economic conditions that collectively shape how individuals currently in the early stages of adulthood might think and behave. Millennials inhabit a world that is unique in several important ways, specifically in terms of its uncertainty, evolving conceptions of work and hyperconnectedness (by this I mean a society in which being connected to devices is our default state; to spend time in person with others is to be "offline," temporarily disconnected from technology).

These conditions provide us with a framework from which it is possible to address the particular, that is, specific persons and situations. It is a deliberate choice on my part to focus on philosophical concepts in this book rather than to make extensive use of surveys, polls and other forms of empirical data. As such, going forward I will refrain to the greatest extent possible from referring to millennials, and instead focus on the conditions that can help us address particular circumstances.

To think in terms of data or evidence often comes at the expense of philosophical reflection, which I believe is badly needed on this general topic, and in society more broadly. Neglected in so much of the public conversation about the "future of work" is moral reflection, in which we consider what kinds of things we should value, how values should be prioritized, what kinds of lives are worth living and so forth.

It might surprise us that John Maynard Keynes viewed the study of economics as a means to living "wisely, agreeably, and well."[3] Similarly, the economic historian R. H. Tawney considered economics to be a branch of ethics rather than the predominantly mathematical and robotic pursuit that it has since become. For many reasons society has become very hesitant to engage in the kind of moral discussion that Keynes and Tawney endorsed, opting instead for a relativism in which it is enough to respect individuals' preferences, tastes, wants and desires—whatever these might be. This book is certainly informed by social scientific study and personal observation; however, a lot of my thinking relies on the work of several prominent moral thinkers of the twentieth century. This sort of philosophical approach, as far as I know, has yet to be adopted in much writing about the "future of work."

The argument put forward in this book is that solitude is for the millennial generation an ignored though ultimately vital practice, conducive to leading rich and purposeful lives as individuals. Solitude has been forgotten in modern life. Our propensity for action squeezes time that we could otherwise dedicate to solitude. We pursue potential but without really thinking about what all the striving is actually for. This in turn wastes a lot of energy and minimizes the potential impact that many of us care so much about.

Solitude, I argue, is not just a matter of disconnecting, of seeking temporary relief from the time we spend online. It is a practice in which individuals can better formulate questions pertaining to their lives as well as listen carefully to their responses. Few of us realistically engage in this, even though it helps us answer the kinds of personal questions that fundamentally shape the lives that we lead. In other words, there is a certain sense of self that can be cultivated in solitude and that is difficult to grasp otherwise.

Fundamentally, solitude is a practice through which a person can better understand their identity, using as material what they hear and see in the hustle and bustle of modern life. From this place, a person can make sense of experience in their *own terms*. I highlight *own terms* for a reason: so much of the identity that I see among this generation is really a rapid but thoughtless piecing-together of views conducive to self-expression that conforms to whatever is socially accepted.

Despite the many resources for self-expression at our collective disposal (social media platforms, for instance), few of us express ourselves *authentically*, that is, in ways that reflect who we are and what we actually think. I find there is a false seriousness in this generation. Many appear to be "purposeful" on the surface, though I often doubt how serious these purposes really are when push comes to shove. I suggest that universities are particularly to blame in this problem—that their emphasis on producing adaptable and employable graduates has contributed to countless graduates entering the workforce with only a faint sense of what they believe and care about.

I come at this book from several perspectives. First, I am a member of this generation, and I have spent the last four years interviewing friends and colleagues in similar life stages across their twenties and thirties. Through my previous company, I worked with clients across multiple industries primarily in Canada and the United Kingdom, and following my exit from the company collaborated with additional organizations in the United States and Israel.

Over the course of this work, it became apparent that something is severely lacking in the language used to talk about our life aspirations (and that is used, more generally, in much contemporary analysis about work and education). Specifically, terms such as "wants," "needs," and "desires" frame our discussions about living a good life. We place a lot of our trust in people's preferences—that ultimately, we must respect what our colleagues want and not ask too many questions (especially when it comes to what should be valued in life and how we should conduct ourselves).

Employers want to know how to satisfy millennials' wants, needs, desires and aspirations. Of particular importance to universities is ensuring that students graduate with "skills" that can help them achieve their aspirations. Nowhere in these conversations is much consideration given to commitments that transcend the individual. For the friends and colleagues whom I speak with, there is, not surprisingly, a tremendous anxiety to perform, to progress in life and to achieve notoriety. This urge to perform is the be-all and end-all for many, whether we acknowledge it or not.

In talking about this generation and its goals, the individual usually comes well before society. This is apparent in the ever-growing number of leadership networks offered to millennials. These networks are geared toward high-potential individuals, those who have achieved "success" in the early part of their lives and who seem destined for bright futures. I have been part of several of these groups, with these experiences coloring my later commentary in the book. Many of these networks focus on creating local "impact," but I have in my own experience in these networks come to see much of the impact-driven activity as a means for members to broadcast themselves *as they wish to be seen*. Put differently, much of the activity in these networks leans more toward promoting oneself than it does toward actually being of service to others in a tangible way.

I also approach my writing as a member of the academic community. Past graduate work brings a philosophical lens to my commentary on this demographic, inspired by the likes of Charles Taylor, Robert Skidelsky, A. N. Whitehead, R. H. Tawney, Adam Phillips and others. A philosophical lens is, as I have previously stated, a missing thread in contemporary discourse about modern work.

I would be remiss not to consider a final perspective in the genesis of this book, which is that *I*, as a millennial, sometimes struggle with hyperconnection, a propensity to *do* at the expense of reflecting on what the doing is for. I find that individuals with strong views on a particular subject often tend to behave in their private lives in a manner contradictory to their stated beliefs. Often these contradictions go unnoticed, or simply unmentioned, by these enthusiastic advocates and authors, though in rare instances they are made explicit.

David Brooks for instance, in his book *The Road to Character*, acknowledges that as a pundit, much of his career has been in the limelight, in which fame is won at the expense of meaningful relationships.[4] This seems to have inspired Brooks to write about the need to place relational values above individual fame and achievement in his writing. In this sense, my focus on solitude is partially a result of grappling with this practice in my private life. The tension has been the source of considerable reflection and conversation with peers over the past years.

Many of my colleagues—no matter where they are located—seem interested in solitude. Many even long for this in their lives. Yet most have a difficult time dedicating the sort of time and space needed for this practice, as it runs counter to what they feel will get them ahead in their careers. Solitude, however, is not antithetical to progress. Rather, it is a means through which our progress can be more richly reflected on. The speed and immediacy in our hyperconnected world provide us with the ability to self-reflect quickly but only superficially, and because of this, we are likely to forget that the development of a rich vocabulary about the good life *should*, in fact, take time.

## WHY FOCUS ON MILLENNIALS?

I have already briefly addressed this question, but will now elaborate in more detail. The book focuses on this generation for several reasons. First, millennials are entering the workforce at a time in which significant technological change is occurring. This is the first generation confronted with the challenge of navigating online *and* in-person identities just as they transition into the workforce and begin their careers. Online lives being a recent phenomenon, this transition is one of heightened awareness of performance and identity, particularly as it pertains to one's career. The creation of a "personal brand," for example, is facilitated through online life. Indeed, the lines between online and offline identity have blurred, such that there is considerable debate on what kinds of identities are most authentic.

A second point pertaining to technological change involves the nature of comparison among this cohort, which I believe is the source of considerable anxiety in our day and age. A variety of reports, for instance, suggest this is an especially lonely generation despite its supposed connectedness. Modern life allows for a lot of thinking as to *what else we might be able to do* in our lives. We glorify choice. We have greater access than ever to other people's stories. And we place a lot of value on how we express ourselves in the various dimensions of life. I would imagine that constant intercomparison impacts mental health, more adversely than positively. Comparison is, after all, a gateway to loneliness.

Third, there is much discussion among millennials about achieving things like purpose, meaning or impact in our work. Not surprisingly, there is an entire industry built on the facilitation of *purpose*, especially in major cities like London, New York and Los Angeles. These organizations are in some ways laudable in that they attempt to help people enrich their lives. But much of the thinking produced in these companies is pretty conventional, and we should hesitate when any consultant—no matter how qualified in positive psychology or a similar field—enthusiastically tells us how we, *as individuals*, can find meaning.

Fourth, it is important to note that the public discourse on millennials splits along two very different lines of thought. In the first case, one focused on affluence. In the second, one focused on precarious work and bleak futures. These narratives sometimes mix together. In this introduction, we have so far dealt primarily with the former (and this will be the case for most of the book). Much of the current writing in this area assumes that the population already meets a particular socioeconomic threshold conducive to its members being able to comfortably weigh options before making choices.

But we must consider this second narrative: that of a generation caught in a cycle of low-pay, unstable work, in which participation in particular rites of passage (such as marrying or buying a house) is delayed well beyond the times at which their parents engaged in these same activities. *The Guardian* is here notable for its reporting on this topic, highlighting for instance that "a combination of debt, joblessness, globalisation, demographics and rising house prices is depressing the incomes and prospects of millions of young people across the developed world, resulting in unprecedented inequality between generations."[5]

I can think of several friends and colleagues who, despite graduating with advanced degrees from prestigious universities, only found suitable employment more than one year following their university graduation. These individuals worked hard to find jobs. If these sorts of individuals struggle to find work outside of, say, the retail industry, then there is reason for concern. A key challenge, then, in the conversation about millennials is in deciding *which groups* we are actually referring to. In this book, I focus mostly on individuals with the good fortune to have pursued postsecondary (i.e., university or college) studies. Readers should thus be aware of the limitations in my approach. However, these two narratives do sometimes intermingle. Indeed, many holders of undergraduate degrees struggle to find stable employment even if their prospects are on the aggregate superior to those without comparable forms of education.

## THE STRUCTURE

This book is divided into three parts: Part I, entitled "Work and Careers"; Part II, "Hyperconnectedness and the Networked Life," and Part III, "Solitude, Aloneness and Loneliness." Each of these parts consists of three chapters. In Parts I and II the focus is on the conditions that individuals face as they come of age. Part III addresses the topic of solitude based on the challenges outlined in the previous sections.

In Part I, I focus on the key problems that drive the compulsion to do more that is so characteristic of this generation. This begins with an account of the integral role that work plays in forming an identity in our society. Following this, I examine the relationship between skills and wisdom in modern work, the former being the concept that dominates how we now think about the aims of education. Finally, I focus on the rise of precarious work in society—not only materially but also psychologically—and then on the problems that this creates for many of us as we reflect on important questions related to who we are.

In Part II, I shed light on the topic of progression. In the first chapter, I outline research on hyperconnection in society, and on the consequences, both positive and negative, that this has on workers. In the second chapter, I examine several of the major networks to which millennials aspire to gain entry, namely, the Global Shapers Community, which is an initiative of the World Economic Forum. There is no shortage of networks for "young leaders," "changemakers," and "social entrepreneurs," and I believe that the proliferation of these labels and networks tells us something important about how we think about progression within modern careers. In the third chapter, I focus on the ways in which social comparison and success stories in media publications influence expectations as to the ways in which lives and careers will develop.

In Part III, the discussion turns to solitude, as one would expect given the book's title. The first chapter consists of an exploration of loneliness and aloneness, two concepts that should be examined prior to considering what solitude means. The second chapter focuses on solitude, outlining the qualities and feelings—such as patience, frustration and a sense of the private—that I believe are vital to it. In chapter three, I address several potential counterarguments to solitude, which fall under categories of access ("Who can spend time in solitude?"), community ("Does solitude weaken community?")

and education ("Should we advocate for solitude at the same time as educational institutions demand that students compete with each other and for jobs?").

I should note once more that it is *not* my aim in this book to provide readers with solutions pertaining to millennials. I am not going to debunk anything or give pointers on how to optimize work productivity among young staff. Readers are really best to develop their own strategies here. My aim is rather to illustrate the conditions that I believe most shape work-lives for those coming of age, and which together serve as a basis upon which readers can arrive at their own conclusions, specific to their own particular circumstances. I argue strongly in favor of solitude, which I believe can help restore integrity in our inner lives in a way that many of us are yearning for. If this book is successful, then it will help readers set aside time and space for solitude, and through this more clearly formulate and answer personal questions conducive to leading rich lives as individuals.

## NOTES

1   Adam Phillips, *Missing Out: In Praise of the Unlived Life* (London: Hamish Hamilton, 2012), 1.
2   Sherry Turkle, *Alone Together* (New York: Basic Books, 2011), 3.
3   Robert Skidelsky, *Keynes: The Return of the Master* (London: Penguin Books, 2009), 55.
4   David Brooks, *The Road to Character* (New York: Random House, 2015).
5   Caelainn Barr and Shiv Malik, "Revealed: The 30-Year Economic Betrayal Dragging Down Generation Y's Income", *The Guardian* (March 7, 2016). Available at https://www.theguardian.com/world/2016/mar/07/revealed-30-year-economic-betrayaldragging-down-generation-y-income.

# PART I

# WORK AND CAREERS

# CHAPTER 1

# THE SPIRIT OF WORK

When arriving at London's Heathrow Airport, one thing always grabs my attention. The HSBC advertisements, which cover the jetway walls right after disembarking from flights, capture so effectively the role of work in the fabric of our daily life. The advertisements are simple, each touching on some facet of an individual's "personal economy." One advertisement reads, "We focus on the most important economy in the world. Yours." Another states, "It's not just leisure, it's part of your personal economy." These and other related HSBC advertisements are as frightening as they are ingenious. They show that this is an age in which work is central to how we define ourselves. We see ourselves as mini-economies, in which we must invest in order to maintain our skills, productivity and competitiveness. It is for this reason that the HSBC advertisements are so powerful.

In the modern world, what matters is that a person is working (this usually refers to gainful employment) and is busy in this work. It is better to have a job than to be without one, whatever this job might be. In other words, individuals must be occupied, taking action, for this signals value. Conversely, the idea of a person sitting alone, not doing anything, is interpreted as being unproductive—and in turn not good for the wider economy. Recent research suggests that millennials are firmly rooted in this work culture, this being a generation that forgoes leisure in favor of long hours. *Harvard Business Review* editor Sarah Green Carmichael notes that "according to a new survey by Project: Time Off and GfK, Millennials are actually more likely to see themselves—proudly—as 'work martyrs' than older workers, and less likely to use all their vacation time."[1]

A risk in work martyrdom, of course, is burnout, and here the *Financial Times* management editor, Andrew Hill, provides astute observations on millennial work culture through reflection on his experiences beginning as a trainee journalist. Hill argues that millennials should approach their work with modest aspirations, for some recent research that he cites suggests that viewing work as an intense calling raises the likelihood of burning out. The most successful of employees, in Hill's experience, "did not put work at the centre of their identity, or treat their job as a world-changing mission. As a result, they kept their zest for the job alive long after others had had their spark snuffed out."[2]

We can situate these two commentaries in a broader historical context, notably through the writing of the late German sociologist Max Weber in his classic book *The Protestant Ethic and the Spirit of Capitalism*. Weber indicates that in the past, work was valued as a moral calling, one that ultimately served God. However, in recent centuries, as the role of religion in society has diminished—and as people have become increasingly dismissive of moral language—work has become an end in itself. For Weber, "It is true that the usefulness of a calling, and thus its favor in the sight of God, is measured primarily in moral terms, and thus in terms of the importance of the good produced in it for the community."[3] However, he acknowledges that "material goods have gained an increasing and finally an inexorable power over the lives of men as at no previous period in his history."[4] As a result, "the idea of duty in one's calling prowls about in our lives like the ghost of dead religious beliefs."[5]

Weber laments the fact that work in his time had lost much of its moral underpinning. As the significance of religion declined in Europe, individuals continued to work diligently but without clear moral purpose in their efforts. Today work remains central to individuals' lives, but is really just a matter of employment. We see work through an economic rather than a moral lens: we need to create jobs to grow the economy rather than ensure these jobs provide individuals with dignity. Weber's analysis rightly suggests that work alone cannot illuminate the human soul. Work needs a larger narrative.

Martin Luther, the German theologian whose relentless efforts in the early sixteenth century gave rise to Protestantism, provides us with some valuable historical background. Born on November 10, 1483, in Eisleben, Germany, Luther received his doctor of theology degree in Wittenberg in 1512, and would over the course of his life produce books, treatises, pamphlets and translations in a way that resembles the kind of output that we in today's world see from a person like Elon Musk.

Of particular relevance for our discussion on work is Luther's thinking about *vocation*, which laid the groundwork for much of society's current thinking about work, 500 years later. Luther argued that *all* Christians have vocations. This served as a break from previous Christian thinking on vocation, in which only priestly callings were considered to be vocational activities. Luther's innovation had several effects. First, it leveled the playing field between contemplative and active lives. Prior to Luther's work, the contemplative or spiritual life had been seen as the higher form of living—spiritual activity was accorded special value. By saying that *all* Christians have a calling, Luther put the life of worldly activity on equal footing with the spiritual life. He argued that a person's worldly calling came through their various stations in life, say, as a husband or wife, as a son or daughter, as a butcher, as a maid, as a scientist or whatever other roles they assumed.

This meant that part of one's duty toward God consisted in fulfilling responsibilities within their various stations in life. With this, Luther provided his followers with a sense of vocation *in the world*, but these vocations also limited their ability to progress (in the sense of social mobility), for a vocation was really just a reflection of the roles given to individuals based on their birth. To do something other than what the stations into which a person was born asked for would have violated the worldly calling. However, the innovation remains, this very rough sketch outlining how Luther instilled significance in a person's nonspiritual work.

Protestants built on this understanding of worldly vocation with considerable intensity. As Weber notes, the restlessness with which Protestants carried out their work represented an ethos—it was their way of life. Moreover, as Protestants gathered wealth in their worldly activity, they saw it as their duty to *continue* to reinvest capital in order to ensure ongoing activity in the world. The Protestant ethic favored restlessness over stillness, though crucially with a moral purpose in mind.

Rational conduct, without emotion, was central to Protestants' approach to work. As this approach "began to dominate worldly morality, it did its part in building the tremendous cosmos of the modern economic order."[6] The restlessness tied to this ethic certainly resembles how we think about work in modern life. Yet, there remains a critical distinction between then and now. The Protestant ethic was ultimately a *moral* calling; work was not an end in itself. This is a key distinction between Weber's conception of the Protestant ethic and our modern conception of work.

The calling as Weber describes was ultimately a religious and ethical activity, aimed toward the fulfillment of a purpose that went beyond the individual. He described work lacking a broader moral structure as living within a *cage*, and based on this he wondered how ethical direction might be recovered. He was certainly on point in his reflections, yet little has changed since: nearly one century later, we are unable to respond effectively to Weber's concerns. Millennials are a particularly intense manifestation of this. Many are work martyrs, but without necessarily considering what, beyond their personal fulfillment, work is really for. Indeed, work provides many of us with purpose, but far too often focuses more on the self than on a broader moral vision. We can examine several examples for further insight into what I mean.

## FINANCE AND CONSULTING

There is perhaps no better example of identity residing in work than for many of those in the consulting and finance industries. Companies in these industries generally feed on recruits with "high ambition and low conviction," a phrase I first heard several years ago, and which I believe is accurate in describing what kinds of individuals tend to flock to these industries. This is not to say that there are not good reasons for pursuing jobs with the likes of Morgan Stanley or Goldman Sachs. Rather, I am continually amazed by how quickly the supposed "critical thinkers" of the world—whose undergraduate studies we would assume develop these abilities—surrender themselves to jobs based mainly on status and remuneration. What we see here is the Weberian account of the cage in full force: most of these individuals wind up deeply unhappy with their jobs, and with a weak sense of why they pursued them in the first place.

In her *Yale Daily News* article "Even Artichokes Have Doubts," the late Marina Keegan attempts to understand why it is that approximately 25 percent of Yale graduates enter the finance and consulting industries. Her reflections spurred in part by a McKinsey & Company e-mail she received at the end of her second year of university, Keegan interviews a variety of Yale students pondering these options. Keegan writes that interviewees' reasoning goes something like this: "Eventually, I want to save the world in some way. Right now, the best way for me to do that is to gain essential skills by working in this industry for a few years."[7]

These companies emphasize how, through working with them, it is possible to improve personal skills and in doing so develop the capacity to one day change the world. The excellent pay, of course, also piques students' interest and puts pressure on students interested in more uncertain forms of work (such as the arts) to begin considering these options. Additionally, time—the short two- or three-year commitment to these jobs—helps justify a person's decision to pursue a line of work that is for most opaque at best.

We can tie Keegan's comments back to the earlier HSBC example. In thinking of ourselves as individual economies, we limit the language for thinking about who we are to a matter of human capital, that is, we think in terms of our *skills*. More specifically, we think in terms of how these skills can be marketed. By spending two or three years in a consulting firm or in a large bank, we imagine that we will develop skills that can then be leveraged for jobs in other, more meaningful, places. The two or three years are then viewed as a sort of personal investment. And so we become less fearful of thinking about the opportunity costs in pursuing things that, for the majority of us, do not align at all with what we actually care about in the world.

As a graduate student at the University of Cambridge, I was at first surprised to see so many gifted, curious and hard-working students gravitate toward these industries. It seemed that, although intellectually curious, a significant portion of students lacked social autonomy. In other words, they were largely unable to listen to what their peers had to say, sit on what they heard and then decide where they, *as individuals*, stood on the question of what kind of life is worth leading. It was not so much that they would enter these two industries that surprised me, but rather that they would do so without much prior careful thinking.

This issue is not unique, however, to Cambridge. I have seen this with groups of high-achieving students at the University of Alberta, where I pursued my undergraduate studies. One of the real challenges that gifted and hard-working students face is simply that they are smart. As a result, they are able to perform psychological gymnastics in which they rationalize why entering an industry such as consulting, about which they know nothing, really *is* the right path for them.

It is hard to reason with these individuals, as most construct compelling arguments as to why they really should join a bank or consulting firm postgraduation. Their decisions are framed as a matter of preparing themselves for the long term: "I will do three years in consulting, then several years in a hedge fund, then a few years in private equity, and after all of this, I will be able to give back to the city in which I was born!" But their overarching purpose in the long term remains unclear. This is the logic that many individuals fall back on, given the lack of moral vocabulary at their disposal for thinking about meaningful work.

Two additional interpretations might work in order to explain why millennials enter these sorts of industries. The first is that many of the supposed "best and brightest" of this generation are actually just really good box-tickers. Stated differently, the people who put themselves in positions to enter blue-chip firms are the kinds of people who try to check every box conducive to enhancing their social status. In addition to their close-to-perfect grade point averages

(GPAs), they compete in several sports, serve on the executive teams of various university clubs and lead some sort of "tech company."

A related interpretation is that this generation is a coddled one, its members considered special by their parents and given highly structured schedules as children. Thus, many delay adult responsibility as they explore themselves through a developmental period now referred to as emerging adulthood. Parents helicopter above, ready to step in whenever called upon to solve their kids' problems. In both cases, people follow structures set out for them, without really taking ownership of their lives as responsible adults.

There is, I believe, a lot of truth in each of these narratives, even though each ignores important structural considerations. What I mean by this is that the behaviors described above might be, in some important ways, beyond individuals' control. They are not completely responsible for their problems. As growing numbers of young people participate in some form of higher education, the reality is that there is now increasing competition for good jobs. Moreover, competition for good jobs takes place not just on domestic but increasingly on global levels.

Given this intense competition for jobs, why *wouldn't* parents equip their children for success in education and, following this, in the labor market? Moreover, how could students not take advantage of the opportunities provided to them by their parents? Indeed, the higher education system into which young people enter is one where considerable emphasis is placed on nonacademic activities, in large part because millennials know they must pursue every possible opportunity to set themselves apart from their numerous age-mates also likely to have undergraduate or graduate degrees. Over time, the standard for expected accomplishment at a relatively early age rises, until nearly every person tends to be involved in some form of fancy leadership activity.

A final, no less important and related interpretation is that today's learners are simply not provided with many educational experiences in which moral language is used. As high school students and later at university or college, seldom do individuals engage in serious conversation as to the sorts of lives that are worth living and the kinds of people that they wish to be. On these important topics, they are left to fend for themselves; conversations and debates take place within the confines of student dorms, in fraternity or sorority houses, or tangentially as part of student club activities. Naturally, these conversations are exploratory—though no doubt entertaining—and so most lack guidance from individuals with much greater life experience and wisdom.

In my experience, this is a real problem, and we can forgive individuals if they graduate from a university or college without having reflected systematically on these critical life questions. Engaging with these questions is of course hard for *anyone*, even with encouragement. It is especially difficult to do so on one's own. Apart from several exceptions, the vast majority of millennials whom I know lack this sort of moral vocabulary. They have never learned it, and the places where we should expect this to be learned—schools and universities—generally fail to provide much of lasting value.

This is part of the reason, I think, that so many Yale (and other!) graduates sleepwalk into the finance and consulting industries without knowing what these jobs really entail. It is not that the students in Keegan's article are unaware of the fact that consulting probably *isn't* the kind of work that they really care about. Rather, many individuals simply do not possess the moral foundation from which they can think critically and confidently about who they are, what kind of people they want to become and what they want to do in their lives. When confronted with dozens of recruiters, even the most intellectually curious individuals falter. One might be intellectually autonomous and yet lack the moral basis from which real freedom, as I see it, develops. In other words, it is possible to be clever without necessarily having much conviction and commitment to things beyond the self in its narrow sense.

Educational institutions are, in large part, at fault for their negligence here. Having bowed to the economy—the primary aim for universities nowadays is to ensure that students develop the skills required to meet evolving employer demands—universities through their words and actions show students that they should really only look after their personal economies. Thankfully, special professors do exist. These are the kinds of professors who shape the lives of hundreds if not thousands of their students and serve as a counterbalance to all of this. But I fear that this sort of wisdom will diminish over time within our university walls as this generation passes on.

Until modern work is thought of in terms of broader, moral purposes, we cannot expect that people will think much differently about why, and for whom ultimately, they work. This is not to say that many or even most individuals do not question their decisions to enter industries such as finance and consulting: a variety of recent articles show that finance and consulting, though for many years the two leading destinations for the graduates of top American business schools, are losing ground to other industries in their share of recruits. In response to this, banks provide their employees with new opportunities, such as short-term placements with nonprofits.

Within finance, there is promise in that several industry leaders are beginning to make important strides in fostering moral thinking. The Governor of the Bank of England, Mark Carney, is a prime example of this. In a 2014 speech entitled "Inclusive Capitalism: Creating a Sense of the Systemic," delivered at the inaugural Conference on Inclusive Capitalism, Carney highlights the significance of social capital within the finance industry. Specifically, he says that "finance has to be *trusted*."[8] Carney remarks that "to counteract this tendency [toward market fundamentalism], individuals and their firms must have a sense of their responsibilities for the broader system."[9] The industry must think about *who* it serves, in human terms, and that values such as fairness and trust must be nurtured over time. This begs important questions: "Who does finance serve? Itself? The real economy? Society? And to whom is the financier responsible? Herself? His business? Their system?"[10]

Carney is among the leading financiers of his generation: a former Goldman Sachs star who transitioned from his private sector role into leadership with the Bank of Canada. His success in Canada, particularly during the financial crisis, contributed to him becoming one of the most respected financial leaders in the world. In his career, it is clear that Carney's work in finance has been undertaken with social and moral aims firmly in mind—a characteristic that sets him far apart from his peers. He dedicates considerable thought to the ways in which financial policy affects the life of the average citizen, and particularly the poor and vulnerable. In his speech cited above, for example, he highlights the reality that "inflation hurts the poor the most and the real costs of financial instability—unemployment and the seizure of credit—are likely to be felt most acutely by the poor."[11]

If more senior leaders such as Carney speak publicly about finance as a *vocation*—that finance is a profession in which there are particular responsibilities beyond the self—then we would have much less to worry about in seeing large portions of talented and hard-working individuals embark on these given paths. Certainly, these industry-level dialogues take time. There is also no industry or company that is morally perfect. However, there is a definite need for young workers, their employers and educational institutions to think about what their work is ultimately for—morally and socially. Especially in finance and consulting.

## MILLENNIALS AND MEDICINE

While the working hours in finance and consulting are significant, even they do not compare to what is expected of physicians. The brutal work hours expected of young physicians have rightly captured the public's attention in recent years, the Stanford Department of Emergency Medicine providing a particularly interesting response to physician burnout. Detailed in the *Washington Post*, the program allows physicians to bank the time they spend on underappreciated work, such as mentoring, which they can then transfer to other services—such as support in their academic research and grant writing—in their personal or professional lives. According to research highlighted by the newspaper, "Doctors, on average, work 10 hours more a week than other professionals, with nearly 40 percent working 60 hours or more."[12]

The stories of young physicians currently in the early stages of their careers can help us better understand the challenges they face in medicine. Among the most compelling of such testimony is that of Lisa Pryor in her *New York Times* op-ed "Doctors Are Human Too," in which she comments on colleagues committing suicide, the prevalence of depression and the inability of physicians to voice their struggles for fear of being considered weak or unfit for medical life.

> The job of a doctor in training is unspeakable. It is hard to find the words to describe what we do. It is hard to work out whom to tell. We cannot speak of these things to people outside medicine because it is too traumatic, too graphic, too much. But we cannot speak of these things within medicine, either, because it is not enough, it is just the job we do, hardly worth commenting on.[13]

The above passage is representative of what appears to be a desire among early-career physicians to speak publicly about their struggles in the profession. On Facebook, many of my friends and colleagues in the medical profession frequently share articles focused on their mental health, the work hours, rampant bullying and sexism from senior physicians and, more frequently of late, suicides taking place among young physicians. Not long ago, the young Canadian physician Robert Chu committed suicide after being twice passed over during residency matching.

It is commonplace to say that reform is needed within the medical profession, particularly regarding work hours. Still, some physicians argue that a 36-hour shift provides residents with the breadth of experience and grit required to become full-fledged members of the profession. In the article highlighted above, an interviewee notes that when beginning his medical career, physicians were given the mantra "Work more. Live less."[14] This mantra is more explicit than the clever HSBC advertisements discussed at the beginning of this chapter, though the implication in both is similar: that we ought to measure the significance of our existence based on our work output. Rather than measure the ability of a doctor based on their bedside manner, empathy and ongoing care for their patients, what matters is that they are endlessly productive.

Millennial physicians differ from their professional colleagues of previous generations in their extensive use of social media. Rather than keep their medical experiences to themselves, they are keen to express these in public forums. They are not reluctant to share with the public their struggles in medicine, wishing instead to educate the public as to what their day-to-day lives entail. Only last week, a medical student at my alma mater wrote an op-ed—disseminated widely through social media—about her struggles with depression as a medical student and the need for more students to embrace and discuss their personal challenges with colleagues.

Only 20 years ago, such open discussion would have probably been unthinkable. Conversations about medical culture would have been limited to hospital corridors. Millennial physicians have, in past years, been vocal in their misgivings about the profession, and media outlets certainly lend a hand in sharing their stories. The ridiculous work hours aside, however, one cannot help but wonder whether young physicians overstate the gravity of their situations as professionals.

After all, entering medicine is a *choice*, one that should require some awareness of the sights, smells and difficult conversations that physicians inevitably face. Though none of the above examples is enviable, it is the *manner* in which these issues are often put—and this is reflected in my anecdotal observations with friends and colleagues in medicine—that concerns me. There seems to be a hypersensitivity to dealing with real-life ethical issues, a subtle unwillingness to subject oneself to the process required to assume responsibility. This is not to dismiss the importance of conversation, particularly in public forums, about issues such as mental health. It is rather that so much of the concern that I see in the medical profession borders on being a request for sympathy right when young physicians assume professional responsibility.

Many years ago, I attended a high school in which many 15- or 16-year-olds had already somehow decided that they would pursue medical careers. Based on this and later experiences, I find that a significant portion of the millennial physicians whom I know enter the profession for two primary reasons: social status and pay. Seem familiar? This is of course very much like the previous finance and consulting example. Often it is the parents, rather than the prospective physicians themselves, who make these decisions.

Clearly, no 15-year-old knows what medicine entails (unless, of course, one of their parents or siblings is a physician), and yet they want to enter medicine at this early age. They work relentlessly to succeed in their high school examinations and gain entry to a medical program. Many of my former high school peers are now physicians. Throughout their university years, few seemed to waver from this single path. Ever committed to their studies, these students finished with near-perfect GPAs, extensive extracurricular involvement and, in many cases, several years of undergraduate research experience in medical laboratories.

Of these friends and colleagues, a few became truly self-reflective and curious individuals over the course of their undergraduate studies. The majority, however, were academic automatons, focused primarily on optimizing their chances for entry into a Canadian medical school. Many were successful in their goals, but I cannot help but wonder whether these individuals ever stopped to consider why *they* wanted to become physicians.

This was reflected in a recent consulting project that I led, in which one of Canada's major faculties of science worried, based on their anecdotal observations, that growing numbers of their students view their science undergraduate degree only as a path to medicine. Given that only several hundred spots per university per academic year are offered for medical entrants, most aspiring physicians are ultimately unsuccessful in their medical school applications. This leads to identity crises. One interviewee, in particular, struggled when thinking about herself as being something other than a physician: "So for me, it was personally very hard to consider another option for a long time, because once I set a goal for myself, I really need to achieve that goal in order to feel self-satisfaction."

Millennials, by and large, lack the moral language conducive to thinking about what kinds of lives—rather than careers or jobs—are worth leading. Hence, they become narrowly focused on goals like medical school, with no vision as to what else might be worthwhile in the world. In other portions of this interview, the interviewee remarked that it was difficult for her to break the mold as one of the only individuals in her friend group to decide that medicine was in fact not the right path for her. Decisions such as these require courage, and it is admirable that this interviewee was capable of sensing and acting on her intuition that medicine might not be right for her.

These decisions are particularly difficult when few individuals think in terms other than achieving career goals, a mindset that is usually based on finding jobs with prestige and good pay following graduation. When prestige and pay are leading drivers, medicine (in the Canadian context, at least) becomes an obvious possibility. Universities are once more to blame, providing little encouragement for their students to think in broader terms than in practicing time-management skills, providing seminars on workforce opportunities or developing so-called soft skills geared toward the workplace.

## THE SEARCH FOR BALANCE IN WORK

An alternative to relentless work is finding *work-life balance*. When thinking about millennials, this brings to mind images of yoga, cycling trips and remote work in exotic locations. Work-life balance says that we are much more than our jobs. When work becomes too busy or stressful, other activities must provide the necessary respite. On the surface, work-life balance seems to make sense. It is a clean idea that assumes that we should never spend too much time dedicated to a particular cause, for we must carefully maintain our well-being.

But work-life balance is a problematic term in several important ways and requires examination given its prominence in society. The term goes too far in the opposite direction of the preceding examples. Yes, there are certainly occasions where a person's relationship with work does them more harm than good. A person becomes single-minded in the pursuit of a particular goal, to the point that relationships with friends and family, physical health and other important parts of their lives begin to deteriorate. Work becomes the sole object of attention and, in turn, produces stress that stultifies thinking.

These, however, are never clear-cut situations. We should expect that anything really worth pursuing might require some sacrifice and thus discomfort in the present. The challenge with balance is not only that it is too obvious a term—one that conforms to the lightness characteristic of modern life—but also that it gives us an easy escape route whenever we feel especially stretched in our work.

Public discourse about work often reduces the term to work as gainful employment. Put differently, we tend to make the error of seeing work as our *job*. However, work takes many forms, and a considerable amount of work is undervalued in society when it does not result in getting paid or provide some other form of recognizable economic benefit. (For instance, the work of a single mother or father is an important kind of work, especially if this single mother or father is industrious in their efforts to provide their children with opportunities that they might not themselves have had. This is an important form of work, but it is usually not valued in society.)

Work-life balance is, perhaps, a reaction to this very thin interpretation of work as employment. A broader conception of work would instill meaning in tasks that are for the most part not recognized as being of much significance in society—at least in comparison to our careers—and contribute to fewer individuals searching for meaning through a vague conception of balance.

When work aims toward ends that transcend the self, this contributes to transformation in the world, as well as in the self. When we believe that work is a matter of service and engage in this work with few distractions, the self is often forgotten—but in a way that empowers us. Our minds are quieted. Indeed, when partaking in this kind of work, the self taps into sources of wisdom that cannot be accessed through mere balance. The turning inward of the self in the name of well-being or safety that balance implies can never be a source of true empowerment, for it is only through sacrifice in pursuit of a moral cause that the self is enriched. Balance cuts off the possibility of this sacrifice, preferring instead protection from discomfort.

When we undertake transcendent work, the richness that we feel reaches into our very being, even if the work feels like a sacrifice in the present. This richness provides us with the vigor needed to address parts of our lives that we might have been suppressing (and that we wrongly feel can be addressed through balance). Conversely, when we feel lost in our work—that it is not for us, that it is disconnected from things of real significance to us—this dampens other parts of our lives. Work framed in purely economic terms usually does this to us. Balance only prolongs our misunderstanding. It forgets that work instilled with moral purpose enhances the self.

In sum, the notion of work-life balance demonstrates that our societal relationship with work is corrupt. Recalibration in this domain is paramount. Work-life balance serves as an indicator that we as a society must put moral aims on par with the economic aims. A collective vocabulary pointing beyond the self must be retrieved. It follows that we should not turn away from the need to sometimes sacrifice the self for causes greater than ourselves. The sense of a calling described in the work of Max Weber, for instance, would enhance the currently limited view of work as mere employment.

Many of us, I think, sense this need to change course. Balance, however, as a solution is really just a matter of escapism, of disconnecting when in fact deeper responses—such as sacrifice—are needed. Band-Aid solutions, such as company sports tournaments or exercise classes might be fun in the moment, but these kinds of activities leave us wanting. Better solutions point beyond the self—they tie our work to sources of richness, wisdom and warmth that individuals are unable to access purely on their own, no matter how productive their personal economies might be.

## NOTES

1   Sarah Green Carmichael, "Millennials Are Actually Workaholics According to Research," *Harvard Business Review*, August 17, 2016. Available at https://hbr.org/2016/08/millennials-are-actually-workaholics-according-to-research.

2  Andrew Hill, "Unrealistic Expectations Put Millennials at Risk of Burnout," *Financial Times*, May 9, 2017. Available at https://www.ft.com/content/be3289be-2c3e-11e7-bc4b-5528796fe35c.

3  Max Weber, *The Protestant Ethic and the Spirit of Capitalism* (London: George Allen & Unwin, 1930), 162.

4  Ibid., 181.

5  Ibid., 182.

6  Ibid., 181.

7  Marina Keegan, "Even Artichokes Have Doubts," *Yale Daily News*, September 30, 2011. Available at http://yaledailynews.com/blog/2011/09/30/even-artichokes-have-doubts/.

8  Mark Carney, "Inclusive Capitalism: Creating a Sense of the Systemic," *Bank of England*, May 27, 2014: 3. Available at http://www.bankofengland.co.uk/publications/Documents/speeches/2014/speech731.pdf. Emphasis in original.

9  Ibid., 3.

10  Ibid., 8.

11  Ibid., 4.

12  Brigid Schulte, "Time in the Bank: A Stanford Plan to Save Doctors from Burnout," *Washington Post*, August 20, 2015. Available at https://www.washingtonpost.com/news/inspired-life/wp/2015/08/20/the-innovative-stanford-program-thats-saving-emergency-room-doctors-from-burnout/?utm_term=.ef87285c1acc.

13  Lisa Pryor, "Doctors Are Human Too," *New York Times*, April 21, 2017. Available at https://www.nytimes.com/2017/04/21/opinion/doctors-are-human-too.html.

14  Schulte, "Time in the Bank."

# CHAPTER 2

# MISUNDERSTANDINGS OF KNOWLEDGE AND SKILL

One year ago, I served as a panelist at a conference for several hundred high school teachers in Alberta, where one of the main questions was, "What must schools do to prepare young people for the workplaces of today and tomorrow?" The panel originally intended to focus on the idea of skills. As part of our preparation as panelists, we were given a *Forbes* article entitled "The 10 Skills Employers Most Want in 20-Something Employees," which lists traits such as the ability to work in a team, technical knowledge related to a job, computer skills and the "ability to sell and influence others."[1]

The panel was, fortunately, a success, in that the panelists largely ignored the question of skills in favor of a more enriching conversation about the ways in which teachers can alter the trajectories of their students' lives through the simplest of gestures and encouragements. It was a heart-warming occasion. However, the topic itself, and its focus on a high school audience, struck me. The concept of skills now prevails in modern thinking about education. This emphasis, which has been developing for many years, implies a reductionist view of what it means to be a human. Value is attributed to the things that a person is able to *do* and how they are able to market themselves.

The skills discussion is framed within larger narratives, such as that of the "Fourth Industrial Revolution" recently developed by the World Economic Forum and its founder, Klaus Schwab. Through these stories, we arrive at a point where it is taken for granted that a good education involves the development of skills, to be of use for employers and workers in their careers. Moreover, through this emphasis on skills training, we lose touch with wisdom, which implies the use of knowledge with *style*. I do not believe that we should entirely reject public discourse on skills—it can be of value depending on how it is framed—but the skills conversation through a predominantly economic lens has already gone much further than it should. It numbs the minds of those that care about improving the world.

## SKILLS AND SOCIETY

Among the most prominent of skills narratives is that of the World Economic Forum's Fourth Industrial Revolution, released as part of the 2016 edition of the World Economic Forum Annual Meeting in Davos, a gathering of many of the world's prominent CEOs, political leaders and celebrities. In his article "The Fourth Industrial Revolution: What It Means, How to Respond," Schwab highlights the velocity of current technological innovation. This is a world in which the "possibilities of billions of people connected by mobile devices, with unprecedented processing power, storage capacity, and access to knowledge, are unlimited."[2] Schwab highlights the importance of artificial intelligence and notes that job losses could disproportionately affect those with low rather than high forms of skill.

Schwab, I think, is correct in many of his assessments. Now on the minds of many policy makers, business people and academics, technologies such as artificial intelligence could pave the way for job automation across multiple industries. This in turn poses enormous policy challenges for governments. For Schwab, the Fourth Industrial Revolution will have a variety of human repercussions, in that it "will change not only what we do but also who we are. It will affect our identity and all the issues associated with it: our sense of privacy, our notions of ownership, our consumption patterns, the time we devote to work and leisure, and how we develop our careers, cultivate our skills, meet people, and nurture relationships."[3]

Governments publish a seemingly endless barrage of reports on skills and the future of work. The number of skills plans and reports produced in recent years by governments, think tanks, universities and trade associations must count in the hundreds, if we are to look at documents created in Western nations. For instance, the British government in July 2016 released its *Post-16 Skills Plan*, which presents an "ambitious framework to support young people and adults to secure a lifetime of sustained skilled employment *and* meet the needs of our growing and rapidly changing economy" (one cannot write a skills report without highlighting at least once the reality of "rapid change in the twenty-first century"!).[4]

Not to be outdone, Canada's federal government launched an Advisory Council on Economic Growth, which in February 2017 produced a report entitled *Building a High Skilled and Resilient Canadian Workforce through the FutureSkills Lab*. From the outset of the report, we encounter the reality of a "rapidly changing economy," one that "will have a profound impact on the nature of work and jobs of the future."[5] Referencing reports written in the United States and Australia focused on skills and modern work, the advisory council finds that "Canada currently lacks an overarching strategy to deal with the increased probability and scale of job dislocation, and must help prepare Canadian workers for the skill demands of the future economy."[6] Most skills reports are similar: they say that given the changing nature of the world, governments, businesses and universities must collaborate in order to better prepare graduates for uncertain futures, in which a dynamic set of skills will be required in order to thrive regardless of the obstacles thrown people's way.

When one begins to press on what these skills pronouncements really mean, however, one begins to see that really, the answer is *not much*! Large consultancies and "thought leaders" trade on these reports. But more often than not, the skills highlighted in these documents include the ability to work in teams, communication skills, work ethic, creativity and the ability to sell others on ideas. They suggest that disciplinary knowledge matters, but only to an extent; the real test of a person is that they are able to adapt to "unforeseen circumstances." These skills narratives are rather pedestrian: we are told to problem-solve, collaborate or communicate, but with little sense as to what any of these things actually means.

Looking critically at these lists, we really have to ask: what do we find so special about these skills? How are these skills different from anything that we have been doing in the past? Of course, there are particular skills, such as sales, that might not come naturally to a person and that need to be taught. But why has so much ink been spilled on the topic of skills, particularly when the skills highlighted in government and business reports are for the most part dull and predictable? For governments and universities to think of themselves as skills producers, when in fact the skills commonly highlighted are unequivocally uninspiring, indicates a deeply troubling vision of what we as a society envision for our young people.

Numerous people, as we have seen, have grown up with this sort of educational philosophy—if we can even call it that—guiding their instruction, and so it should perhaps come as no surprise that career anxiety exists in this generation when thinking about finding purpose in work. Their education so narrowly conceived, they have little of lasting value in their moral vocabulary to ruminate on when faced with uncertainty.

## ENRICHING OUR UNDERSTANDING OF KNOWLEDGE AND SKILL

We are in need of an enriched account of skills. Specifically, we must better outline the relationship between skills, knowledge and wisdom. We can here turn to the work of one thinker in particular, the mathematician-turned-philosopher and theologian, Alfred North Whitehead. In his book *The Aims of Education and Other Essays*, he provides us with insight into the relationship between wisdom and knowledge. Whitehead's thinking about the stages of "romance," "precision," and "generalization" in learning lays for us a solid groundwork for our reflection on the above topics, one that deepens rather than deadens the soul.

Though first published in 1929, Whitehead's ideas are illuminating for current discourse about knowledge, wisdom and skills. Missing from contemporary discussion about knowledge is a sense and appreciation for what knowledge can be for, beyond application toward technical problems—the study of which is usually undertaken in the name of progress, productivity, competitiveness or some combination of these economic aims. Instead, Whitehead suggests that knowledge must be related to the *life* of the person in possession of it: namely, "What education has to impart is an intimate sense for the power of ideas, for the beauty of ideas, and for the structure of ideas, together with a particular body of knowledge which has peculiar reference to the life of the being possessing it."[7]

The possessor of knowledge must demonstrate precision and restraint in its handling, which Whitehead calls *style*. For Whitehead, style "pervades the whole being [...] [and] is the ultimate morality of the mind."[8] It is not all that is required in the possession of knowledge, though, as what matters first is that a person is able to achieve his or her desired end: "The first thing is to get there."[9] Whitehead calls this *power*. But it is a person's style in the possession of knowledge that helps solve a given problem with limitation of waste.

Later in his book, Whitehead describes the process by which knowledge develops an active quality, that is, in which it becomes wisdom. Evoking images of much modern university education, he prefaces his discussion with the assertion that "the drop from the divine wisdom, which was the goal of the ancients, to text-book knowledge of subjects, which is achieved by moderns, marks an educational failure, sustained through the ages."[10] Wisdom, for Whitehead, consists in "the handling of knowledge, its selection for the determination of relevant issues, its employment to add value to our immediate experience."[11] Wisdom is a marker of the *freedom* of a person. He proceeds to describe the cultivation of freedom in its threefold process, this characterized by romanticism, precision and generalization.

In this first step, the stage of romance, a person demonstrates interest in a particular area of study, for without this interest one cannot progress. The role of the teacher is paramount in cultivating this interest, in that the teacher helps instill in a student excitement in the object of study. Some wandering in this stage is to be expected. After this, we move to the stage of precision. Whitehead warns against pushing a student too far in the learning of particular facts and theories. Yet, "there is no getting away from the fact that things have been found out, and that to be effective in the modern world you must have a store of definite acquirement of the best practice."[12] Put differently, Whitehead remarks that "there are right ways and wrong ways, and definite truths to be known."[13]

The stage of generalization consists of "shedding details in favour of the active application of principles, the details retreating into subconscious habits."[14] It is in this stage that a person continues to utilize laws, rules, principles and theories, but does so without conscious reflection on their utilization. In this stage, what matters is "who has the knowledge and what he does with it."[15] Through all of this the role of the wise teacher is paramount, in that the teacher guides a student along a path in which discipline and freedom are in constant tension.

If only our contemporary educational "gurus" could provide us with the kind of enjoyment that we experience in reading Whitehead! Though written nearly one hundred years ago, Whitehead's educational philosophy is timely when thinking about modern work, education and the experience of today's young people in all of this. He shows that skills and knowledge are valuable only insofar as they enhance the life of the being. Without such connection, they are inert, lacking in meaning.

Furthermore, Whitehead rightly shows that we must *commit* ourselves to particular traditions of thought in order to develop robust knowledge, our predecessors being critical players in our personal formation. The Whitehead overview helps counter the idea that we must simply be "adaptable" in a rapidly changing world (a topic I will soon address). Instead, it is through commitment to particular bodies of knowledge that a person is, ironically perhaps, most likely to thrive in chaos.

## RESISTANCE TO BODIES OF KNOWLEDGE

One of the dominant ideas that we now encounter in universities is that non-academic studies matter as much as—if not considerably more than—academic studies. The time spent within a classroom is seen as superfluous in the modern world, with students believing that they learn much more on their own, through self-study, student government and club activities, and whatever else it is that they do in the community. Universities, ironically, give tacit assent to this philosophy, through the growth of nonacademic services such as entrepreneurship (or start-up) education.

In my experience, this was particularly the case in the political science department, where students skipped large numbers of classes in order to spend time working with political parties or campaigning for positions in student government. Many of these students were convinced that their academic studies provided them with little if any utility. Why sit in a classroom listening to a professor, or read books, when a person can learn everything by actually *participating* in the things being read about? Why not simply take action?

Lack of interest in committed study is not just true in political science; this impatience occurs across the university. In their well-known book *Academically Adrift: Limited Learning on College Campuses*, Richard Arum and Josipa Roksa survey undergraduate students across several dozen American universities and colleges and discover that undergraduates typically only study 13 hours per week, half as much as was the case in the 1960s.[16] This seems about right to me. There are exceptions—the rigor of particular programs, such as mathematics, physics or engineering usually require that students spend more time than this exploring and studying in order to grasp the material presented to them—but in general one of the major challenges in modern education is that of sustained commitment to learning.

The vast majority of people that I've interviewed over past years do not believe that it is worthwhile to spend time in a classroom, for academic commitments require trade-offs with more exciting and fulfilling activities. There are many reasons for this shortage of patience. I will give four of them.

The first pertains to the size of classrooms in modern higher education. In classes of 100 or more students, there is little opportunity to interact meaningfully with a professor. This suggests to students that it is not even worth going to class. The second is that of laptops within classrooms, which detract significantly from the quality of discussion in the seminar room or lecture hall. When students are on Facebook or YouTube, the reality is that their attention is not on the professor. This lowers the quality of interaction between class participants. The third challenge is that of a growing belief in the power of the autodidact, in which students believe that they are capable of teaching themselves well enough. Why listen to a teacher when the knowledge is already out there online? The fourth reason, as I have seen in past years, is that of the variety of demands placed on students as they move through the university. As the price of undergraduate education increases, many students are forced to balance their studies with jobs and other commitments needed in order to keep themselves afloat.

More generally, there is a certain attitude that affects individuals' dispositions toward academic learning. This is the modern propensity to *express* oneself, which is facilitated through time spent on social media. Millennials see the university less as a place in which they should be informed than as a playground for the expression of their preexisting values and beliefs. Most are not interested in reading unfamiliar authors, because doing so would challenge what they already believe to be true.

As I reflect on my time as an undergraduate taking political science and philosophy courses, there were perhaps two or three professors—and certainly no more than three dozen students—who reflected seriously on their beliefs, pursuing their studies beyond what was expected of them in the classroom. Not surprisingly, these students would assemble outside of class hours, at the pub or in coffee shops, in order to carry on their conversations.

Why is there so little time for committed learning? Why the lack of time and respect for traditions? Why the lack of value given to our collective past? The advent of social media, and the reality of the "tethered self"—a term coined by Sherry Turkle, which we will examine in Part II—make it difficult for millennials to engage in the three stages of learning that Whitehead describes. It is nowadays extremely hard to critically examine a body of knowledge in a precise and extended manner. Attention spans are far too short, commitments too weak and distractions too plentiful for much detail.

The fact of the matter is that in modern life, individuals can *get away* with this sort of superficiality, their self-expression on social media—and the affirmations they receive—providing them with the sense that what they have to say actually matters. Whether or not a person is informed, there is nowadays always an audience. This deludes us.

Another reason for this shallowness is that distrust exists between young people and their elders. There is a growing belief in the power of youth. Without question, this belief has positively impacted the world in many ways. But it also sidelines elders and their wisdom. The democratization of technology, in which ever-greater technologies are made accessible to anyone, provides many people with the ability to innovate despite their relative youth. Contributing to this sense of possibility for youth are scholarships such as the Thiel Fellowships, in which extraordinary young people (under the age of 20), receive $100,000 to drop out of school and work on start-up ventures. These sorts of things suggest that young people needn't listen to their elders; they can make it just fine on their own.

All of this supposed power transferred to the young brings with it great expectations and a profound sense of disappointment when the young fail to measure up to what they believe they can or should be doing. Indeed, to expect success at a very early age causes anxiety as one wonders whether one is doing enough. It is a mindset of impatience. This is one of the unforeseen consequences of the "age does not matter" attitude. In my observations, the millennials with this attitude—and there are *many*—believe that because age does not matter, they must constantly outdo themselves because the sky is the limit. As they approach their thirties, they begin to wonder what their lives have really amounted to.

To be 30 means that a person should have already accomplished something of significance in their life. Working backward, a millennial in their mid-twenties should obviously be well on the way to some spectacular achievement. At first, believing that age is not a barrier to accomplishment seems inspirational (and it certainly can be). That said, as we dig further into the implications of this attitude, it becomes apparent that this is a double-edged sword. This attitude is conducive to thinking bigger and testing personal limits, but also reminds us of what has not yet been achieved.

I do not mean to imply that with age comes wisdom. This is far from always the case. That said, in general wisdom results from life experience and thus to a large extent from age. This is a reason why the elderly have much to impart to the young (though in Western society we seem not to recognize this very well). Much greater value should be given to relationships involving the imparting of wisdom between a teacher (in their various forms; not only in educational settings) and a younger person. My concern, based on past observation, is that many of us tend to dismiss, or are simply unaware of, the importance of this kind of hierarchical relationship. Rather than embrace opportunities to examine knowledge within the context of others' more extensive lived experiences, we wonder what it is that an older person could ever really show us.

One might immediately object by saying that mentorship is an activity of enormous interest to young people in the early stages of their careers, in addition to the practice of sponsorship within companies. However, I have trouble with the instrumental manner in which mentorship relationships are often framed. While necessary, mentorship programs too often focus primarily, or exclusively, on how a person can progress in their career. In my experience, as well, the individuals who consider themselves mentors—and say so explicitly, for instance through interviews or websites—are probably *not* the kinds of wise individuals to which Whitehead refers in his book. The truly remarkable mentors are, in my experience, not really mentors, but "older friends." To make explicit mention of mentorship in a relationship between the old and young tarnishes the relationship itself.

Two such older friends play formative roles in my own life (and those of many others). It is worth briefly describing them in order to better illustrate what I mean by relationships with the wise. Surely many readers have their own examples. In the first case, I think of a professor in political philosophy who, in his forty-plus years of teaching, has shown countless students what it means to do philosophy, that such an activity is worth doing, and that regardless of what a person does or becomes in life, philosophy shall always matter. I first heard of this professor through several colleagues while working in the student union, and so decided to reach out to him at the beginning of my third year at the university. The professor responded, saying that it might in fact be possible for me to participate in a semester-long Aristotle seminar focused on the *Nicomachean Ethics*. This seminar would prove formative: it is among the reasons why philosophy has become an important part of my life.

But the philosophy seminars were merely the starting point in countless students' friendships with this professor. Seminar conversations often moved into local pubs following the conclusion of evening classes. And many students, myself included, continue to meet as frequently as possible with this professor in order to discuss philosophy and other questions related to the university, provincial and federal politics and life more generally. Telling is the fact that many former students, several of whom have become leading political figures across Canada, return as frequently as possible to participate in these philosophy seminars.

What I think most students value over the years is the sheer breadth and depth of experience that this person brings to his life. His zest for life shapes the way in which students think about philosophy, so much so that many students pursue this for their careers. Indeed, in spending time with this professor, one simply knows that one is given a rare opportunity to learn from the fascinating experience of another human being and, more specifically, from the experience of a person who has lived *well*. Time spent in the presence of a person who lives well offers a glimpse into what it means to be knowledgeable in an active sense, where knowledge informs a particular kind of *being* in this world.

The second example pertains to a business leader who, though retired (in theory, at least), continues to work tirelessly to provide young Canadians with life and career opportunities that recognize their hard work and dedication to their communities. I met this person for business advice soon after the creation of Gen Y Inc., my former company. From our first conversations he shared perspective that shaped my understanding of business as a *vocation*. This person began his engineering career in Canada, and following studies and several years working in London, returned to Canada, eventually becoming the chief executive of one of North America's largest oil companies. In his time at the helm of this company, he contributed significantly to the growth of Northern communities and supported the creation of Aboriginal businesses whose annual output is now in the billions.

As with the previous example, in my coffees with this individual, it is abundantly clear that the conversations provide the opportunity to learn from a person who has lived well. Though I might not remember the exact details, the stories shared about his engineering work on the River Thames, his negotiations with workers and unions, and the setting-up of successful nonprofit organizations serve as material for ongoing self-reflection. To this day, in serving on multiple boards, this individual recognizes and rewards the talents of young people, and does so with a discipline and purposefulness that inspires. His efforts have resulted in Canadian millennials meeting the likes of Henry Kissinger, Larry Summers and Madeleine Albright in recent years, spending days with them in intimate conversational settings. Every discussion with this person is to be cherished, for it provides the opportunity to listen and learn about what it means to do something well.

So why are individuals averse to this kind of teacher-apprentice relationship? A contributing factor is that modern life dismisses the past, which is reflected through the use of terms such as self-actualization. Self-actualization takes place in the present or future, and makes little reference to the past. Case in point, the number of books published in recent years on future forecasting is astounding.

We celebrate our future leaders and put faith in the *next generation* of talent. To spend time with people whose successes were in the past would be a violation of this inclination to focus on the future. After all, a rapidly changing world puts an expiration date on knowledge—only present knowledge can seemingly be usefully applied to the world's problems.

Moreover, for many, living in the present means engaging in activities that do not demand much commitment. The self exists in the *now*; attachments only slow a person down. Unfortunately, cultivating the kinds of relationships described in the above examples is time intensive. Wisdom is revealed in layers, through ongoing interaction with a person over a period of *years* rather than months. (This is another reason why mentorship programs are not representative of the relationships that Whitehead describes: they are too structured, often with time boundaries of six months or one year that outline when meetings with a person begin and when they end.) This constitutes, to borrow the language of the Jewish philosopher Martin Buber, an "I-It" rather than "I-Thou" relationship.

Appeals to be present oriented or authentic are usually tantamount to narcissism. They are a reflection of a person's desire to avoid commitments, under the false assumption that to not commit oneself to someone or something ensures freedom. But freedom emerges when a person dedicates oneself to a particular activity, through which a grasp of fundamentals inherent in the chosen activity can be developed. It is only through commitments that we develop genuine freedom.

A second reason that underlies hesitance to spend time with older people is cultural. Western culture attempts to push older people out of sight and therefore out of mind. We associate older individuals with sickness, slowness and a lack of skill (or skills that no longer apply to the world). We assume that past life experience is no longer relevant to the realities of modern society, and that their skills cannot possibly be useful, considering the technological innovations occurring so quickly in our ever-evolving world. These attitudes are reflected in the idea of a retirement age, which the philosopher Martha Nussbaum rightly considers to be one of the leading social injustices of our time. In short, belief in progress, through its implicit focus on "applicable" knowledge, risks that we dismiss the elderly.

For those who spend time with the kinds of older friends described in this chapter, it very quickly becomes apparent that mental sharpness is usually in no short supply. Moreover, relationships with the wise demonstrate that despite society's incessant chatter about progress, the world changes much, much more slowly than we imagine. (Whitehead, though having written in the early 1900s, provides us with material that is not only relevant to modern education but also delivered *more eloquently* than any contemporary educational commentator I know of.)

Wisdom is intergenerational. Our openness to it is influenced by our conception of time. A narrow view of time leads one to assume that the only time that matters is that of the present era, in which technological breakthroughs are believed to change the world. This leads us, often unconsciously, to dismiss the past and in turn sweep away the individuals who cultivated their wisdom in this past.

A longer view of time, in contrast, shows that many of the world's critical problems regarding poverty, education and inequality were often of equal significance to philosophers, politicians, business figures and other members of society of decades or centuries past. Accordingly, it helps to reflect on our individual time horizons, as these horizons can determine our respect for the past and, thus, of our elders.

Finally, to partake in these sorts of relationships requires that young people ask *questions*, the responses often demonstrating to interlocutors that their understanding of the world is limited. Freedom takes place not when individuals discover and express their own values, arrived at through their independent searching, but instead, through immersion within a particular language or system larger than themselves. By this, I mean things like communities of practice, scholarly traditions or faiths—each with their own histories, norms and unique demands that shape human action. I will discuss these in a later section.

It is through curiosity and dialogue within these kinds of systems that individuals overcome their own narrowness. TEDx talks come to mind as being particularly representative of the inability to listen that I see among a large portion of millennials, which only perpetuates our narrowness. The TEDx talks by so-called life coaches and many young "changemakers" are a case in point: few are that insightful! Many of these individuals think that what they have to say is of significance and desire a stage for sharing their "thought leadership." I will get to this later.

Unfortunately, inquisitiveness runs counter to one of the main "twenty-first-century skills" previously discussed: that of *selling* others, of showcasing oneself. Millennials are led to believe that it is important to sell themselves, which we see through the prominence of the term "personal brand." The personal brand suggests that we are each supposed to be known for something distinctive, and that we should put some effort into displaying this distinctiveness in our in-person and online interactions. This is reflected in how we carefully curate social media profiles and go to the trouble of building personal websites. To develop a brand requires personal expression, in which a person reflects on their values, skills and personality, and thinks about how these can be *packaged*. The key is to showcase these things to an audience.

This packaging demands an internal questioning process: "What are my values, skills and personality traits, and how do I make sense of them?" in the first instance, and "who is my audience?" in the second—but it is an exercise ultimately geared toward sharing for approval. This kind of sharing seeks external validation. The wise relationship described in this chapter involves the opposite. The aim here is not to express oneself, but rather to listen and consider what it is in one's self that might be incorrect, flawed or otherwise deficient. This usually requires some thoughtful breaking down of the self in relation to wisdom. One must take in and *consider*, rather than project.

## ADAPTABILITY

The last factor impeding the cultivation of active knowledge is the modern focus on adaptability, which universities espouse as one of the primary qualities that graduates should develop. Why adaptability is important in university graduates (and young professionals) should now be of little surprise. The narrative goes something along the lines of "the world is changing faster than ever—industries are rising and falling—and so we must not teach students anything that is not directly applicable to the workplace." The narrative then continues: "We need instead to ensure that students learn how to adapt, which we can teach through entrepreneurship, this helping them to 'fail fast,' iterate, and respond quickly to whatever obstacles come their way." It is expected that students will do much more than just sit in classrooms and listen passively to whatever their professors have to say.

Adaptability requires that students do not spend *too* much time in any particular field, sampling instead from as many subject areas as possible. Adaptability at first glance seems innocuous. But as we press into it, we should begin to wonder whether individuals actually lose something in all of this focus on preparing themselves for perpetual change. My sense is that a significant portion of today's students and young professionals, feeling the pressure to be adaptable, enter the workforce having spent four years in higher education building little more than a brittle structure upon which to situate their knowledge.

Yet adaptability is a thin notion. It is weak. It assumes that variety is superior to specialism or depth, given the pace of change in the world. Adaptability is an appealing line of thinking given the world we believe we live in, but it is mistaken.

The business community is, not surprisingly, the leading voice on the topic of adaptability. Employers assert in their various reports that young people are not adaptable enough for the economy they will enter. Far from being dismissed, the liberal arts are heralded as providing graduates with the adaptability required in our uncertain world. In the *Globe and Mail*, for example, the Canadian business leader Brad Ferguson remarks that "we also need interdisciplinary liberal arts graduates to bridge gaps and make sense of incredibly complex systems all around us that aren't necessarily powered by numbers, science and logic."[17] In the past, I was sympathetic to this emphasis on adaptability, particularly in relation to the liberal arts. "Of course the liberal arts provide its participants with skills relevant to succeeding in an unknown world," I thought. "What better way could there be to defend the liberal arts than to emphasize its role in helping develop young people to enter the new economy?"

This line of argument is alluring but dangerous. The first reason is straightforward. Arguments made in favor of adaptability—and those made regarding the liberal arts, in particular—are frequently put forward by business people whose ends are primarily focused on the workforce. They have little conception of what else education might actually be for, moral thinking included.

This is not to say that business leaders have no care for morals and ethics—many do—but there is little question that ethics training in business schools leaves much to be desired. As I have argued thus far, we need to begin moving *away* from this economic mindset, as it implies a narrow conception of work as *the* end to which we strive in our lives.

Second, no professor in the humanities would ever say that their philosophical study, for instance, aims toward the preparation of students for the workforce! This is not what adaptability means in the academic realm, nor should it. A professor in moral psychology focusing on philosophers like Immanuel Kant or Hannah Arendt, for instance, believes that learning how to do good philosophical analysis is what really matters. The professor might say that through this kind of work, they engage in dialogue with a community of scholars, enjoy the intellectual pleasure that comes through such analysis and can acquaint students with particular philosophical traditions. All of these are true and important.

This helps us understand why focusing on adaptability is well intentioned but ultimately misguided. Without its proponents realizing, it suggests that universities are, before all else, training schools for the workforce. And unfortunately this is what countless universities are fast becoming. The influence of this modern understanding of the university is such that it prevents other competing views of higher education from even having a seat at the table. Adaptability reinforces the status quo, which aims toward applicable knowledge, right when we need time and space for dialogue regarding the university's moral aims.

On an individual level, the problem with internalizing adaptability as a value is that it makes settling virtually impossible. What I mean by settling is the ability to stay put on a particular project without continuously shifting focus onto something else. Given the fluidity of modern life, millennials are encouraged to focus on completing *projects*. Projects provide individuals with variety and constant intellectual stimulation, with clear start and end points around which experience can be packaged. But this variety provides us, more often than not, with a relatively fragmented and shallow set of experiences. We jump rapidly from project to project and so lose the opportunity to fully digest what the various experiences amount to as a whole.

I have argued that in the modern age, three factors hinder our collective ability to develop the *style* that Whitehead holds in such high esteem. The first of these is the general aversion to spending proper time learning a particular body of knowledge. Prevailing against this sustained learning is a belief in nonacademic work, which is seen as more operative in the world. In Western society, students spend less and less of their time on academic study, and more on activities outside of the classroom. Knowledge not deemed immediately useful is rejected, and so individuals become unwilling to spend time engaging in a manner that allows them to begin to understand and appreciate it.

Contributing to this is distrust in relationships with the wise. Trapped in present-orientedness, we reject the past, living under the assumption that it is better to self-express than to be informed. And finally, I argue that universities do not help their members' situations, focusing on adaptability as the quality to which graduates should aspire. For these reasons we have a very long road to travel in order to restore appreciation for wisdom in society.

## NOTES

1  Susan Adams, "The 10 Skills Employers Most Want in 20-Something Employees," *Forbes*, October 11, 2013. Available from: https://www.forbes.com/sites/susanadams/2013/10/11/the-10-skills-employers-most-want-in-20-something-employees/#2ed24c3e6330.

2  Klaus Schwab, "The Fourth Industrial Revolution: What It Means, How to Respond," *World Economic Forum Agenda*, January 14, 2016. Available from: https://www.weforum.org/agenda/2016/01/the-fourth-industrial-revolution-what-it-means-and-how-to-respond/.

3  Ibid.

4  Department for Business Innovation & Skills and Department for Education, "Post-16 Skills Plan," July 2016. Available from: https://www.gov.uk/government/uploads/system/uploads/attachment_data/file/536043/Post-16_Skills_Plan.pdf. Emphasis in original.

5  Advisory Council on Economic Growth, "Building a Highly Skilled and Resilient Canadian Workforce through the FutureSkills lab," February 6, 2017. Available from: http://www.budget.gc.ca/aceg-ccce/pdf/skills-competences-eng.pdf.

6  Ibid., 2.

7  Alfred North Whitehead, *The Aims of Education and Other Essays* (London: Williams & Northgate, 1932), 18.

8  Ibid., 19.

9  Ibid., 20.

10  Ibid., 45.

11  Ibid., 46.

12  Ibid., 53.

13  Ibid., 54.

14  Ibid., 58.

15  Ibid., 49.

16  Richard Arum and Josipa Roksa, *Academically Adrift: Limited Learning on College Campuses* (Chicago: University of Chicago Press, 2011).

17  Brad Ferguson, "Don't Apologize for Your Liberal Arts Degree," *Globe and Mail*, March 27, 2014. Available from: https://beta.theglobeandmail.com/news/national/education/dont-apologize-for-your-liberal-arts-degree/article17684918/?ref=http://www.theglobeandmail.com&.

# CHAPTER 3

# PRECARIOUS WORK AND NARRATIVES OF UNCERTAINTY

In October 2016, the Canadian finance minister, Bill Morneau, remarked that young Canadians should prepare themselves for "job churn," a statement that provoked the ire of many across the country. Though Morneau recognized that retraining is critical for workers as they navigate increasingly complicated careers—asking, for instance, "How do we train and retrain people as they move from job to job to job?"[1]—his remarks brought considerable irritation.

Whether in Canada or other Western countries, public dialogue on precarious work is characterized by uncertainty, anger and appeals for worker retraining as career paths become increasingly disjointed. In this chapter, I attempt to shed light on the precarious work narrative, which is an important facet of public dialogue pertaining to young people. Specifically, I argue that whether or not work is precarious, the narrative *itself* creates a sense that uncertainty is the "new normal." This makes it difficult for workers to feel comfortable in whichever jobs they are in. The default mindset has become one of insecurity—even for those in well-off circumstances.

## TRUST AND BETRAYAL

Of the publications that report on precarious work, *The Guardian* is unquestionably among the most vocal about its downsides. Whether in this or other publications, we tend to hear from university-educated young adults working in bookshops, retail stores and other low-paying forms of employment that wonder what their university educations actually provided them. Because of their tenuous situations, these interviewees acknowledge that traditional markers of adulthood—such as getting married or purchasing a house—are unrealistic for them. Or, these important life decisions will be delayed well beyond their twenties, at least for those without parents' generous financial aid.

Mark Carney argues elsewhere that the widening of social and economic inequality between generations risks diminishing the social capital required for our trust in capitalism. In his wide-ranging speech on inclusive capitalism, Carney remarks that "within societies, virtually without exception, inequality of outcomes both within and across generations has demonstrably increased."[2] There is no shortage of writing or speeches focused on precarious work. And there is a sense in delving into research on this topic that the long-term, individual-level repercussions could be severe.

Several anecdotal examples from conversations with friends and colleagues show just how damaging precariousness can be. I recall speaking with an alumnus of a top globally-ranked university who recently spent more than one year searching for a decent job following his graduation.

Despite submitting applications to 75 employers, this person received just one interview. Weighed down by the cost of international tuition, this person needed to find a way to pay back the interest accruing on his loan. However, despite his education and considerable work ethic, it was difficult to find suitable employment even in his hometown. In a similar case, another colleague spent nearly one year searching for entry-level research jobs after completing a postgraduate degree in biochemistry, at one of North America's leading institutions in this field. This person spent more than one year in the job application process, eventually moving back home.

I had not expected either of these friends to have such difficulty finding employment. Nor did I expect each to share their stories with me, coincidentally perhaps, on the *same day*. Considering how they graduated from elite universities and had persistent trouble finding jobs, I imagined that others' circumstances must be even worse. Soon after, stories began to emerge of other friends in comparable situations. This is the new reality: few individuals are nowadays that secure in their employment. Even for the most highly educated of millennials, finding a decent job is not easy. This leaves members of this generation feeling constantly on guard and uncertain as to what their futures will bring. This uncertainty is for many the source of great anxiety.

## DEFINING PRECARIOUS WORK

But what exactly *is* precarious work? The short answer is, "It's complicated." For all of the fear about precarious work, there is little agreement as to what it entails. This is not because public and private sectors or academia have not shown interest in the topic.

Quite the opposite, in fact. KPMG, TD Bank, the United Way, Randstad, Demos and a bevy of other institutions all undertake a lot of research into precarious work. Several key themes quickly emerge when we review the research carried out thus far.

Much of the research conducted to date focuses on the *experience* of workers in precarious situations. In Canada, the Poverty and Employment Precarity in Southern Ontario (PEPSO) research group, supported by McMaster University and the United Way Toronto, provides analysis in this vein. In a 2012 report entitled *The Precarity Penalty: The Impact of Employment Precarity on Individuals, Households and Communities—And What to Do about It*, they find that 44 percent of working adults in jobs in urban Southern Ontario experience some level of precariousness in their work life.[3] These individuals tend to have poor health, little access to health coverage (such as dental plans), are frequently stressed about their finances and delay having families. For instance, PEPSO reports that only 12 percent of employees in precarious situations are paid if they miss a day's work, and that only 8 percent of those in precarious employment situations have drug, vision or dental benefits.[4]

A recent report by the TD Bank Group adds to this line of research, focusing on stress resulting from income fluctuation in precarious work. Here, the TD Bank Group finds that 37 percent of survey respondents report moderate to high income volatility over their most recent year of work. Eighteen percent report high to very high income volatility.[5] This translates to approximately five million adult Canadians reporting high or very high income volatility, with another three or so million saying their monthly income can fluctuate by 25 percent or more.[6] This income volatility can be materially and psychologically harmful, as those with such volatility are two to thirteen times more likely to delay buying food or groceries, delay paying at least the minimum on their credit card bill or delay making a student loan payment.[7] Indeed, "for these workers who live close to the edge, a drop in income caused by losing a client, non-payment, an injury or illness, or a family emergency can be dire."[8] This suggests that precarious work takes place when income flows are uncertain. In other words, when a person does not have a steady paycheck.

Independent work therefore merits our attention, since pay in this kind of work (whether high or low skilled) brings uncertain cash flows. McKinsey provides some of the best analysis on this topic, stating that independent workers are defined by three key attributes: exerting control and autonomy over *how much* and *what* work a person undertakes; being paid by task, assignment or sales, often through digital platforms; and finally, working from client to client over short periods of time.[9] McKinsey finds that between 10 and 15 percent of working-age adults in the United States and European Union-15 (EU-15) earn their *primary* living from independent work.[10] But "independent work is not dominated by millennials. While more than half of those under age 25 participate in all countries, they represent less than one-quarter of independent workers."[11] Thus, much of the existing data on independent work suggests that it cuts across generational lines. Why then the focus on young people—those in their twenties and thirties—when it comes to precarious work?

## PRECARIOUSNESS IN THE MEDIA

There are reasons why this demographic is the target of extensive media coverage related to precarious work. First, media outlets that report specifically or in large part on "millennial issues" ensure that this topic remains top of mind for readers. Second, the tendency toward lack of definition in the term lends itself to a belief that millennials are often in *some* form of precarious work, especially in the early portion of a career in which finding secure jobs can be difficult. Third, the rise in property costs across the Western world prevents many individuals from participating in rites of passage as their parents once did.

The media is a contributing factor to the link between this generation and precariousness. Media outlets with strong millennial bents—such as *Vice*, *Vox* and *BuzzFeed*—ensure that the precariousness narrative is top of mind in public discourse related to young people and work. *BuzzFeed*, for instance, published an article entitled "21 Tweets for Millennials Who Are Just Tired of Bullshit," in which readers encounter bleak accounts of millennial life. Among the examples is a tweet that sarcastically reads "'kids these days have it too easy' said that generation that could buy a house on a wage from unskilled work at age 21."[12] Another states, "My generation loves brunch because it's two hours of distraction from the fact we'll never own real estate," with a third proposing that "there should be a millennial [*sic*] edition of Monopoly where you just walk round the board paying rent, never able to buy anything."[13] In response to an *Economist* article called—in all seriousness—"Why Aren't Millennials Buying Diamonds?" a person tweets, "I work at a grocery store."[14] As of July 2017, the *BuzzFeed* article had garnered over four million views.

Second, the term's ambiguity opens itself to many interpretations—and it is unlikely that many will be positive. Precariousness could involve work that does not provide individuals with pay needed to cover basic living expenses. Or it could simply reflect consistent income volatility, whether income is high or low. What are we to make of individuals working on temporary contracts that *are* able to sustain themselves financially, and yet can never look more than several months into the future as far as their projects are concerned? What about millennials who *choose* to enter independent forms of work? Short-term contracts might be lucrative, but they require that individuals constantly search for additional work while undertaking their current projects. There are a number of ways in which precarious work can be broken down, but little consensus on its definition.

Even if there is much disagreement as to its definition, precariousness can exert a psychological toll on people. My sense is that millennials are *particularly* exposed to this. Narratives about automation and a rapidly changing world are gaining momentum just as people in their twenties and thirties begin their careers and consider what jobs are best for them. We constantly hear stories of young people unable to make ends meet. We are used to the story of the educated millennial who settles for a short-term job in a bookstore or retail outlet, or who is forced to work for gig economy services such as Uber or Deliveroo.

Another track is philosophical, the ongoing sense among this generation that something is missing in their lives. This is a restless generation: achieving comfort in a job contributes to a feeling of falling behind. There is a contradiction here. On the one hand, we hear complaints of not finding good enough jobs. On the other, we are fearful of settling into any particular job given the pace of change in the world.

One final issue needs to be highlighted. The cost of housing is indeed a considerable obstacle for millennials as they work and plan for their futures. In metropolitan cities such as London, Toronto and Vancouver, it is virtually impossible for millennials to buy a house unless their parents contribute. In the *Financial Times* article "London Housing: Too Hot for Young Buyers," we learn that a 25-year-old Londoner earning median wage (£29,900 gross) would, assuming particular conditions being met, need to wait forty-one years and five months to save for the necessary deposit on a £250,000 property.[15] This is for the average male buyer; female buyers must wait another nine years on average to afford the deposit.

The reality is that only those in jobs with excellent pay or with family wealth are able to afford property in major cities. My conversations with Londoners over the last three years indicate, definitively, that housing is a core issue for this generation. Indeed, many successful London friends and colleagues in the early to middle stages of their careers have shared with me their immense frustrations around even affording rent. This is especially so for those not working in corporate environments. Compared with their parents at the same age, young people do seem to be in an especially difficult situation, with many wondering when, if at all, they will get on the property ladder.

## SCARCITY AND TUNNELING

Precariousness is more than a matter of millennials not paying their bills on time; rather, it is a *mindset*. Millennials are inundated with news focused on uncertainty, insecurity and the rapidly changing nature of the world they inhabit. They are constantly reminded that they must be adaptable if they are to survive in a workforce in which disruption features prominently. This is an invisible consequence of all of the talk about disruption, where politicians, business leaders and an entire industry of consultants argue that not to innovate is to die. Given these factors, it takes a rich and nuanced sense of self to feel that life is secure. Indeed, for fear of appearing incapable of keeping pace with modern life, precariousness limits individuals' capacity to think beyond their immediate horizons.

In order to better illustrate the negative psychological effects of precariousness, we can turn to the work of behavioral economists Eldar Shafir and Sendhil Mullainathan, authors of the book *Scarcity: Why Having Too Little Means So Much.* In their book, Shafir and Mullainathan define scarcity as "having less than you feel you need," with the shortfall often financial or temporal (related to time).[16] Their research shows that scarcity "captures the mind," leading individuals to focus primarily on their immediate needs and circumstances. Shafir and Mullainathan call this *tunneling*, with the term "meant to evoke tunnel vision, the narrowing of the visual field in which objects inside the tunnel come into sharper focus while rendering us blind to everything peripheral, outside the tunnel."[17] This tunneling levies a *bandwidth tax*, in which individuals have difficulty mustering the energy required over time to meet their needs.[18] In comparison, individuals with *slack*—that is, with more money and time—are able to think more freely about nonpressing needs and questions, without much risk to their well-being.

Scarcity is a mindset. It affects behavior without our knowing it. Often, it leads individuals to appear less talented or capable than they actually are. When a person is faced with scarcity, they might feel lethargic, simply unable to keep up. This person risks being perceived as lazy or incompetent. This sheds light on a key barrier in socioeconomic mobility: those born into wealth, and thus who likely have access to abundant material resources, needn't think *too* carefully about the decisions they make regarding what they will do in their lives. Though material wealth does not make a person's life decisions insignificant per se, what it does is provide the decision maker with additional room for experimentation and error.

In contrast, individuals with less material security feel that they *must* make good decisions, as failing to do so could waste the significant time and effort dedicated to simply *arrive* at promising decision-making points. For some, this pressure can pay dividends, leading individuals to make excellent decisions that allow them to surpass their comparatively privileged peers. However, the pressure can also narrow an individual's perspective and make for rushed and poor decisions. The findings in *Scarcity* provide a sense as to how individuals respond psychologically to financial and time pressures, which is helpful if we assume that precariousness is its own sort of default mindset for members of this generation. Here it is worth highlighting several points, which together provide more detail on what I mean by this mindset.

First, in a supposedly uncertain world, I believe that young people tunnel on the activities they believe can provide them with the clearest added value in their lives. Given the societal value placed on our jobs, as well as the lack of much collective moral vocabulary, individuals double down on *themselves*. They attempt to become more productive and efficient in their work. We see this in the "lifehack" culture, as well as in the growth of the self-help industry over the past decade. Websites are replete with "how-to" articles, providing readers with tips on how they can be more productive, achieve more success in their careers and digest new material more quickly. In following websites like *Business Insider*, individuals are given tips as to how they can become as successful as famous individuals such as Richard Branson, Elon Musk and Barack Obama.

To pause and contemplate, rather than increase productivity, would be antithetical to making progress in a world that demands activity. But a focus on practical activity—to the detriment of independent thinking—is not an entirely new phenomenon, the British economic historian R. H. Tawney having written about this in 1921 (his criticisms center on the English; however, it most certainly applies to other Western nations):

> It is a commonplace that the characteristic virtue of Englishmen is their power of sustained practical activity, and their characteristic vice a reluctance to test the quality of that activity by reference to principles. They are incurious as to theory, take fundamentals for granted, and are more interested in the state of the roads than in their place on the map. And it might fairly be argued that in ordinary times that combination of intellectual tameness with practical energy is sufficiently serviceable to explain, if not to justify, the equanimity with which its possessors bear the criticism of more mentally adventurous nations […] Most generations, it might be said, walk in a path which they neither make nor discover, but accept, the main thing is that they should march.[19]

In thinking about what constitutes a day well spent, most of us will consider how much we have *done*. Though there is nothing wrong with completing lots of tasks on any given day, one must be careful to not get too carried away with to-do lists, which usurp the time and space required for more constructive thinking—the "reference to principles" that Tawney describes. Getting more done does not equal living more meaningfully. Indeed, practical activity is usually *easier* than thinking about whether our efforts are *really* directed to important things in the first place. This latter kind of thinking requires that we confront ourselves, stepping away from the practical activities that consume our attention.

Closely related to productivity is *busyness*, which is equally glorified in the modern world. Remarking on busyness serves as an entryway into conversation, a means for approval irrespective of the value of one's activities. The substance of activity is not what matters to us. The key is to show others that we are not idle, for empty space in a calendar is sinful. We pay little attention to the potential significance of not doing anything. But why does busyness appeal so deeply to us, and why the lack of consideration as to what value there is in sometimes not filling every slot in our calendars? I will briefly address these two questions, and then consider what we gain and lose through perpetual busyness.

Busyness is appealing in large part because of its expressional value. As will be examined in Part II, the self derives much of its significance from its *presentation*. The philosopher Charles Taylor captures this when he writes about the importance of the journey in modern life, where a person sets out to discover the frameworks that give life a sense of meaning or purpose. Taylor writes that "we find the sense of life through articulating it. And moderns have become acutely aware of how much sense being there for us depends on our own powers of expression. Discovering here depends on, is interwoven with, inventing."[20] Articulating our activities requires that we consistently expose ourselves to new things. How else can we express ourselves than through the practical things that we do? With this logic, it makes sense that we busy ourselves with things, this allowing for the collection of material that can be used for our self-expression. The word "curate" here comes to mind, a word frequently used nowadays. We curate experiences in large part so that we can talk about them.

*Substance* of experience matters less than a person's ability to articulate what is experienced (whatever this may be) in a compelling manner. Individuals gravitate toward activities that show how life is fast-paced and exciting. With our perpetual connectedness, this expression takes place online, for others to see, and so the need for being dynamic heightens. Sharing thus provides individuals with a sense of meaning. Conversely, to not have something to share suggests that maybe a person is not living fully enough. We are susceptible to this kind of performance. To extract ourselves from this way of thinking requires considerable courage, the ability to see through masks and refrain from constant self-presentation.

We get away with this behavior in large part because we collectively lack the language to evaluate the activities we partake in. Moral discourse within society is not widely supported, and universities, as we've seen, do not encourage such dialogue with students. Replacing this is the belief that individuals are consumers, that it suffices to respect our choices. In other words, value is placed on choice rather than on what is chosen. As a result, it is difficult to examine what busyness and self-presentation really amount to in individual cases, for the conversation is virtually impossible to have lest we offend someone's preferences.

Thus, far too many individuals are content to accept others' busyness at face value. Busyness then creates more busyness. It becomes difficult to slow down—to collect ourselves—unless external forces do this for us. Millennials (and certainly many others!) therefore get away with busyness, because we are unable or simply unwilling to value activity apart from its expressional value and, second because it is difficult to slow down to the point that we manage to think about *why* something matters beyond its contribution to productivity.

Given the prominence of busyness in the modern world, most individuals know that, by presenting themselves as busy—as leading varied and interesting lives—they will gain acceptance in their social circles. So many people feel, in other words, that they must spend time with other high-achieving, perpetually busy people. Not to act and present oneself in this way is, precisely, not to belong.

This brings loneliness through the sense that one is missing out. That loneliness is felt acutely when one is alone, without a packed calendar, should be of little surprise to us given our inclination to be doing things. This mindset strips aloneness of its potential significance and produces anxiety that makes *not doing* a real test of inner strength.

We now come to the second question posed earlier: "What value is there in *not* filling every slot in one's calendar?" I frame this question in this way deliberately. It is, in fact, not a very good way to consider the significance of being alone, as it assumes busyness to be our starting point. Put differently, one begins by thinking that living with a filled calendar is the default, and that the reasons for not living in this way must outweigh the sense of purpose—however weak or fleeting this purpose might be—derived from busyness. If one begins from a position of busyness, assuming that this is simply a part of life, then it makes "inactivity" very hard.

I have felt this acutely over past years. Living in the United Kingdom, I often try to make it out to the countryside for day hikes, my intention being to spend time alone reflecting generally about my life, what direction I'm moving in, what I should value. Many of these walks are consumed, at least initially, by a sense that I could be back at home, doing work, sending e-mails and writing articles. As the walks progress, such thoughts gradually disappear and I'm then able to enjoy the scenery without thinking about much at all.

The problem is that starting with busyness as a baseline creates a lot of mental static. If we are not careful, we risk seeing aloneness as time *off*—time *not* being productive, *not* making tangible contributions to the world, *not* expressing ourselves or inventing. Our collective relationship with aloneness might be different if we were to think of aloneness as being an integral part of our relationship with ourselves and with others. Aloneness would come prior to—or at least be on equal footing with—busyness. Aloneness would therefore not just serve as a means to recalibrate given our busyness but also as a place from which we can think about what our busyness is really even *for* in the first place.

Busyness also warps sense of time and, ironically, serves as a barrier to excellence in a particular activity. When asked about what I have done at the conclusion of especially busy days, I have trouble responding. My reaction is often, "I really can't remember!" Conversely, on days focused mostly on one activity (say, on writing, on analyzing a particular book or on working diligently with a specific client), it is much easier to emerge feeling that a day was worthwhile, that something substantial was accomplished. When we spread ourselves thin, it is hard to make sense of what actually transpires in a given day. In hindsight, busy days feel empty, having passed quickly but with little coherence.

There is, however, an expectation that in modern life individuals *will* spread themselves thin. Focusing on a given activity for an extended period of time is seen as a risk, as illustrated in the previous discussion about adaptability. One story puts this into perspective. In talking about this issue with a colleague, she recalled how, as an undergraduate student, a friend once asked her how her semester was going. My colleague responded that her time was spent primarily on reading and analyzing fiction, her major being in English. The friend responded with "That's nice, but what *else* are you doing?" But of course my colleague had no answer for this. Her focus was really just on one thing: her English studies. At this point the friend grew slightly confused, not understanding how his conversant was *not* working on other projects. Examples like these are common in the modern world, it simply being assumed that a person will have several projects taking place concurrently. It is therefore startling when a person does not fit this mold.

Busyness steals from us the possibility of solitude. No matter how we spin it, we cannot spend time reflecting purposefully on our lives when we are perpetually busy. Our interactions with others certainly provide us with material upon which we can reflect about who we are and what matters to us. In this sense, practical activity is important.

But we can only meaningfully make *sense* of this material when we are alone, with time and space for ourselves. Otherwise, the questions that lie just below the surface—and that we are usually only peripherally aware of—cannot emerge.

Busyness, in other words, prevents us from asking good questions about ourselves and, in turn, from intentionally orienting ourselves in directions that are true to the kinds of people that we are and that we actually wish to become. Busyness suggests fulfillment, but ultimately provides thin experience upon which we cannot undertake much valuable self-examination.

Without time and space for ourselves, it is difficult to deal effectively with the precariousness common in the modern world. As we have seen, individuals busy themselves with countless activities in order to show how they are keeping up. Much of the value in such busyness derives from a desire to invent or self-express. As Sherry Turkle writes in *Alone Together*, we begin to mistake the performance of identity for identity itself. The need to constantly perform arises partly from narratives of uncertainty about the world, in which we are told that we must be adaptable and resilient in order to survive in modern life. It should therefore be of little surprise that aloneness is ruled out from our lives when such narratives are internalized, for spending time on our own does not provide us with clear, short-term experiences conducive to self-expression.

## ARE THERE ADVANTAGES TO PRECARIOUSNESS?

I have so far been critical of precariousness, arguing that persistent insecurity leads individuals to tunnel on their immediate circumstances (in this case, focusing more intensely on their work). But what about possible advantages resulting from this? It would be unfair to only brush past these, and so I will now address what might be some of the benefits in living with the mindset described above.

The first of these, and which should come as little surprise to readers, is that of entrepreneurialism: living with uncertainty is for many the impetus to do things *differently*, to launch new initiatives partly in order to improve one's economic situation. Millennials are known for their belief in a special type of entrepreneurship—social entrepreneurship—and it would be wrong not to consider the value of this. A second benefit is in the potential for the creation of new institutions, which again, is often discussed in relation to members of this generation, who are seen as wanting to break down existing systems rather than to work within them. Finally, a third benefit is the opportunity for individuals to learn more about *themselves*, testing and better understanding their own limits as they attempt to overcome the challenges in front of them.

We begin with entrepreneurship, which is widely embraced in the modern world. Defining entrepreneurship is complicated: for some, it involves the creation of a for-profit enterprise, whereas for others it is a skill that a person possesses which can be used in a wide variety of circumstances. For the present discussion, I view entrepreneurship as the relentless creation of value given the resources at one's disposal. Entrepreneurship often involves the establishment of an entity—whether for-profit or not-for-profit—though in my view it is more so a disposition toward the world.

Precarious situations can inspire entrepreneurship. There are countless examples of ambitious, gifted and persistent entrepreneurs who set out with little capital, but nevertheless had a clear vision and built successful ventures. Personally, entrepreneurship is an important part of my life: many of the most important life lessons that I have learned over the last years have taken place through running my own company. Indeed, there are few better ways to learn quickly and intensely about something, as well as to potentially make a meaningful impact on the world. However, we must be very careful not to glorify the stories that we tell about entrepreneurship.

Recent research suggests that the "rags-to-riches" entrepreneurship story is often *false* in the aggregate, in that a significant portion of well-known and successful entrepreneurs initially benefit from family wealth. A *Quartz* article highlights the research of University of California, Berkeley economists Ross Levine and Rona Rubenstein, who analyzed the shared traits of entrepreneurs in a 2013 paper, finding that most successful entrepreneurs were white, male and highly educated.[21] Thus, while "there's certainly a lot of hard work that goes into building something, there's also a lot of privilege involved—a factor that is often underestimated."[22]

With this in mind, we can more clearly see that entrepreneurship should not be viewed as an advantage of precariousness without, at least, a fair bit of skepticism. Precariousness can *sometimes* be advantageous as a catalyst for entrepreneurship, but this is certainly not always or even usually the case. In fact, the *Wall Street Journal* article "Endangered Species: Young U.S. Entrepreneurs" highlighted in 2015 that "the share of people under age 30 who own private businesses has reached a 24-year-low."[23] Appeals to entrepreneurship as a means for solving social issues must therefore be treated with caution. Young people are not necessarily creating companies—and seeking impact through them—as frequently as we might imagine.

A second potential advantage of precariousness is that insecurity will spur members of this generation to create new institutions, under the assumption that existing institutions are simply unsatisfactory for building the kind of world that we want. We see young people creating new nonprofits, founding companies and pushing for change in politics and government. But the data related to individuals in their twenties and thirties and trust in institutions is actually quite mixed. On one hand, the Ernst & Young and Economic Innovation Group report *The Millennial Economy* tells us that "millennials — many of whom entered the workforce at the onset of the Great Recession—have very little confidence in America's banks (27 percent), Silicon Valley (27 percent) or corporate America (20 percent). In the midst of police shootings and lax sexual assault sentencing, more than two-thirds of millennials lack confidence in our criminal justice system."[24] Other research says the opposite: that young people trust institutions such as the church and media more than their parents do.

My observations suggest that millennials *are* in fact rather distrusting of institutions, and that many feel comfortable working in nontraditional organizations. My strong sense is that individuals in this demographic absolutely desire better government, better politicians and better companies. This aspiration is far more representative of this generation, in my experience, than their supposed apathy. After all, there are now countless social enterprises, many of which provide founders and staff with the means to financially sustain themselves while advocating for political, economic and social change in existing systems. Many believe that systemic reform in our government is a must if we're to maintain the same collective quality of life enjoyed over past decades. If precariousness is advantageous for the generation, it is probably here, in that it forces individuals to embrace change and launch new projects.

Finally, it can be argued that precariousness is valuable insofar as it provides individuals with opportunities to learn more about themselves—this learning often driven by fear. It is when a person is up against the wall, filled with fear, that they are forced to overcome what was previously considered impossible. This was echoed at a recent Ditchley Foundation conference, in which 200 postgraduates and young professionals across the United Kingdom gathered in order to talk about the "future human." In moderating a panel called "Working Across Boundaries—Leadership in an Uncertain World," I asked the four panelists to describe the major turning points in their careers. Fear was a common part of these critical junctures, this emotion spurring panelists to think critically about what they should direct time and energy toward in their lives. Fear is a great motivator, and insecurity certainly helps channel this.

A mindset shaped by insecurity and fear can be a catalyst for making significant decisions. Yet, protracted insecurity can also do more harm than good for individuals. When individuals feel perpetually anxious as to what they will do with their lives, this can come to dominate their thinking, making it difficult to collect themselves and achieve the composure required to make good, informed decisions. In politics, we often hear that one should "not waste a good crisis." This can also be applied on an individual level: crises, if channeled effectively, can help individuals learn much about themselves and so live according to who they really are. But when persistent insecurity hangs above individuals, they are gradually stripped of the ability to think critically about the long term. Indeed, precariousness removes from individuals the confidence and energy required for meaningful action—and, more importantly, self-reflection—in the world.

## STRIVING FOR IMPACT AT SCALE

It is taken for granted in the twenty-first century that uncertainty is the new normal. Many agree that rampant technological change is bringing about considerable disruption on systemic, organizational and individual levels. For millennials, I have argued that one of the major implications of this is that precariousness becomes a *mindset*. Individuals come to assume that their lives are inherently uncertain and insecure, this belief reinforced by the deluge of mainstream media publications focused on this generation's many trials and tribulations. They begin to see themselves as being underutilized and constantly at risk of disruption within their careers.

The idea of settling becomes unbearable. The only way to move forward is to work harder, demonstrating entrepreneurialism wherever one goes. This activity must be *articulated* to others, this being the modern-day form of "keeping up with the Joneses." Collectively, these and other factors make for a generation of people where only few comprehend what it means to be still and to contemplate. Boredom, aloneness and of course, solitude, are to most foreign concepts.

Before concluding Part I, I want to very quickly highlight two additional issues associated with our modern relationship with work, specifically as they relate to impact. This will help us later transition into Part III. The first issue is that of striving for impact. Specifically, a growing contingent of organizations, such as 80,000 Hours, now exist in order to help young professionals think about how they can generate maximum impact in their work. These organizations guide individuals in thinking about what kinds of careers—say, working in artificial intelligence, medicine or politics—can produce the best possible outcomes for society. This approach is driven in part by the creation of career guides or plans mapped rigorously to long-term outcomes. The second issue is that we slowly *lose* the ability to be alone.

I will begin with impact maximization. A few stories can help show what I mean. The first takes place in England in the winter of 2016. While attending a lecture with a friend to celebrate the work of a distinguished physicist, I met a doctoral student in the final stages of his degree. The three of us got into a conversation about careers, thinking about the trajectories imagined for ourselves in the future. Emerging from the lecture hall following the event, we continued the conversation and soon picked back up on the topic of careers.

In tracing his intended career path, my acquaintance put it as follows: the first several years of his career would be spent in an investment bank or consulting firm, the next few in a hedge fund and, following this, in private equity. Given this pathway, it would then be possible for this person to make a significant contribution to his home country. He estimated his tenure in finance as being in the 20-year range. Only at this point would it be possible to give back to his home country as "impactfully" as possible.

In a different conversation, this time in Berlin, I was given a similar—and on the part of the speaker, an even more unambiguous and self-assured—account of what the first years of the person's life would look like: ten or so years in finance and health technology companies, followed by a jump into British politics. These are but two small examples of what I constantly see with this generation: an intense focus on creating impact, in which there is an attempt to *plan* the various steps required in order to reach the intended end goal. These narratives are so often articulated with confidence: the outcomes seem to be clearly known, as are the paths required in order to achieve the intended impact.

Among the leading proponents of impact maximization is William MacAskill, author of the book *Doing Good Better*. MacAskill is a faculty member at Oxford University, Y Combinator alumnus and prominent speaker. His work in setting up nonprofits such as 80,000 Hours, to which I alluded earlier, is admirable. There are few individuals as capable of wearing multiple hats as effectively as MacAskill. That said, I think there are real downsides to this belief in impact maximization.

The organization 80,000 Hours structures impact as follows on its website: "The larger the number of people affected"; "The larger the size of the effects per person," and "The larger the long-run benefits of solving the problem."[25] Altogether these considerations help a person plan for impact at scale. The organization highlights the importance of considering which problems are neglected in the world, as well as which ones are actually solvable (there being many charities whose work creates more harm than good). One of the major benefits that I see in 80,000 Hours is in how they encourage people to ask questions about what kinds of careers or jobs they will enter. Such questioning is currently rare within universities, as we've seen in earlier sections. Thus, we should applaud the work of MacAskill and his team for their contribution to much-needed cultural change in how universities encourage graduates to at least think about the long term. But there are several weaknesses in thinking about impact, especially in terms of the planning required in order to go about this.

The first weakness is that impact too often becomes the desired end in a given activity; how the activity itself is carried out appears to be of less importance. What matters is that one creates change on a large scale: activities become worthwhile insofar as they affect many people. Not all impact, however, takes place at scale; finding meaning with small numbers of people is just as—if not even more—significant. In my experience working alongside people focused intently on maximizing impact, their rhetoric seems to draw them away from themselves. I cannot really understand what so many of these colleagues *really* mean when they talk about impact or what their real intentions are in a given activity. The complicated process of creating value for others—whether for small or large groups—seems to matter a lot less than rhetoric focused on doing something big.

Second, in focusing on creating impact, individuals risk overestimating their abilities. They lose a sense of moderation and perspective in their work. Millennials are frequently told that it is up to them to "change the world." When participating in gatherings of the Global Shapers Community (a leadership network that I will discuss in Part II), my colleagues and I were constantly told that we must "Keep shaping!"—that is, shaping the world. Too many individuals within this network take the message seriously, believing that they are in fact capable of changing the world. Frequently shared through social media since his passing, Steve Jobs's "dent in the universe" quote reinforces the idea that individuals must strive to create big impacts in their lives. But in encouraging individuals' supposed potential to change the world, this risks creating unrealistic expectations and ambitions, which for the vast majority of individuals can only lead to disappointment and frustration.

Setting out to change the world through impact also lends itself to narcissism, which is a third weakness. There is nowadays a strong belief in the potential of the individual to effect enormous change in the world. This is no surprise to us given the previous discussion in Part I. Too often in my experience, striving to create impact serves more as a performance (that is, as a means for self-expression) than it does as a genuine attempt to improve some specific aspect of the world. In many of my interactions with so-called "changemakers" or "impact leaders," their work is often as much an effort in branding—of trying to fit in with a particular group of people who *seem* to be doing good for others—as it is an intelligent reflection on what parts of the world can and should be improved.

A related but more important difficulty is that highlighting the importance of changing the world leads individuals to forget, or simply look negatively upon, the notion that humans are limited. Creating impact does not happen quickly, nor should it. Meaningful change requires that we think in terms of years if not decades, not months. It also requires that we act collectively.

Focusing on generating impact, specifically at a large scale, seems to be incongruous with our limitedness as human beings. Again, this is not to say that doing good work in the world is insignificant. The opposite, in fact, is the case! Rather, individuals should not expect that impact will come *quickly*, nor should they set out to create large impact as their primary goal. Ironically, perhaps, worthwhile impact is probably most likely to occur when expectations are modest, but where effort is sustained over time. The self-titled "changemakers" of the world tend to miss this important point.

Finally, thinking in terms of impact lends itself to rigid thinking, in which the ends and means are too apparent to the individual. This is just not reflective of how lives and careers unfold. We are not able to foresee outcomes as well as we would like to imagine. We see this in the previous example of the person whose 20-year plan is clearly delineated: following 20 years in finance, this person will finally (!) be able to create his desired impact. Such thinking is misguided, for it neglects chance.

As the renowned Stanford psychologist Albert Bandura writes, "some of the most important determinants of life paths often arise through the most trivial of circumstances."[26] There is little space left for chance when an intended impact, and the often-quantitative measures used to evaluate this, are assumed to be known at the outset of an activity. This removes the inherent mystery in activity, and along with this, strips us of the perplexities and questions that serve as a basis for meaningful self-reflection.

## TIME SPENT ALONE

Several years ago, while walking through downtown Calgary with a friend on a summer morning, I received some excellent news: this friend had, following years of hard work, finally landed a job at an agency that he'd long hoped to work for. And yet, as our conversation carried on, it became apparent that this friend had not taken his eyes off *other* potential opportunities. His rationale? "I think it's still important to keep options open and think about what else is out there." This is not to say that this person was not grateful for his new job—in fact, he continues to work there today—but rather, he was averse to focusing purely or even primarily on it.

Modern life encourages individuals to think in terms of options, aware of the diverse avenues for self-improvement available to them. But as the British psychoanalyst Adam Phillips writes, the myth of potential contributes to constant falling short, haunting individuals as to what they could have done if only they had so chosen. It follows that we believe we must always *take action* to keep options open. Not to be optimizing for mobility is to fall behind and limit future opportunities.

When impact is top of mind for an individual, it becomes difficult to spend time alone without distraction. Time that could be spent in quiet contemplation becomes time spent worrying, feeling anxious as to what *else* one could be doing in order to create impact: the meetings or calls that could be taking place, the tasks or projects that could be undertaken, the new career paths to be experimented with. Aloneness becomes a thing to be avoided, for aloneness only reminds individuals of what they could be doing.

In a fascinating *BBC News Magazine* article, "The Slow Death of Purposeless Walking," Finlo Rohrer writes that wandering on foot as an activity is disappearing. Rohrer laments that "there are many people who regard walking from place to place as 'dead time' that they resent losing, in a busy schedule where work and commuting takes them away from home, family and other pleasures."[27] Rohrer, commenting on how "many now walk and text at the same time," suggests that there *is* value in getting lost—in finding one's own way—but that such independent navigation is coming to an end.[28]

Aloneness is anything but dead time. Despite this, fewer individuals than before in Western society are apparently choosing to partake in activities in which they can be alone, such as walking. Of course, many individuals do not have access to the countryside or to safe neighborhoods. But there are other settings in which aloneness can take place, each of which is infected by the modern propensity to be "on": spending time alone in one's room; taking a taxi ride from one meeting to another without using a cellphone; sitting and reading in a Starbucks café; or spending time in one's room relaxing and thinking.

Organizations such as 80,000 Hours, for example, provide readers with many valuable considerations regarding which kinds of jobs or careers are worth pursuing. This helps recent graduates and young professionals overcome the pervasive empty-mindedness in entering high-status industries such as finance and consulting.

But as Tawney, Phillips, Whitehead and others have stated at various points over the last century, *doing* strains our ability to reflect when no (or very little) time is set aside for aloneness. Given the conditions that shape modern work, the possibility of spending time alone rarely comes to mind— and when it does, it becomes a source of anxiety, given the awareness of what else individuals could practically immerse themselves in that might be of some demonstrable value.

We shall examine solitude as its own concept in detail in Part III. Prior to this, we must investigate a second facet of the modern world, that of hyperconnection and the prominence of networks.

## NOTES

1 Canadian Press, "Get Used to Multiple Careers, Finance Minister Says," *Toronto Star*, October 22, 2016. Available from: https://www.thestar.com/news/canada/2016/10/22/finance-minister-says-canadians-should-get-used-to-short-term-employment.html.

2 Mark Carney, "Inclusive Capitalism: Creating a Sense of the Systemic," Bank of England, 2014, 3. Available from: http://www.bankofengland.co.uk/publications/Documents/speeches/2014/speech731.pdf.

3 Poverty and Employment Precarity in Southern Ontario, "The Precarity Penalty: The Impact of Employment Precarity on Individuals, Households and Communities—And What to Do About It," May 2015, 93. Available from: https://www.unitedwaytyr.com/document.doc?id=307.

4 Ibid., 152.

5 TD Bank Group, "The Impact of Income Volatility on Canadians," 2017, 2. Available from: https://td-capa.s3.amazonaws.com/prod/default/0001/01/2ed95a1a680ea5b78ab53646f1f432f51405bc02.pdf.

6 Ibid.

7 Ibid., 14.

8 James Manyika et al., "Independent Work: Choice, Necessity, and the Gig Economy." McKinsey Global Institute, October 2016, 92. Available from: http://www.mckinsey.com/global-themes/employment-and-growth/independent-work-choice-necessity-and-the-gig-economy.

9 Ibid., 12.

10 Ibid., 92.

11 Ibid., 15.

12 Jasmin Nahar, "21 Tweets for Millennials Who Are Just Tired of Bullshit," *BuzzFeed*, May 16, 2017. Available from: https://www.buzzfeed.com/jasminnahar/tweets-for-millennials-who-are-tired-of-bullshit?utm_term=.hcpwWVWXX#.ye7LWBWmm.

13  Ibid.
14  Ibid.
15  Nathan Brooker, "London Housing: Too Hot for Young Buyers," *Financial Times*, April 27, 2017. Available from: https://www.ft.com/content/a0182e62-25e4-11e7-a34a-538b4cb30025.
16  Sendhil Mullainathan and Eldar Shafir, *Scarcity: The True Cost of Not Having Enough* (New York: Times Books, 2013), 4.
17  Ibid., 29.
18  Ibid., 13.
19  Richard Henry Tawney, *The Acquisitive Society* (London: G. Bell and Sons, 1921), 1.
20  Charles Taylor, *Sources of the Self: The Making of Modern Identity* (Cambridge: Cambridge University Press, 1989), 18.
21  Aimee Groth, "Entrepreneurs Don't Have a Special Gene For Risk—They Come from Families with Money," *Quartz*, July 17, 2015. Available from: https://qz.com/455109/entrepreneurs-dont-have-a-special-gene-for-risk-they-come-from-families-with-money/.
22  Ibid.
23  Caelainn Barr and Ruth Simon, "Endangered Species: Young U.S. Entrepreneurs," *Wall Street Journal*, January 2, 2015. Available from: https://www.wsj.com/articles/endangered-species-young-u-s-entrepreneurs-1420246116.
24  Zachary Crockett, "Millennials Have Very Little Confidence in Most Major Institutions," *Vox*, September 28, 2016. Available from: https://www.vox.com/2016/9/28/13062286/millennials-confidence-in-government.
25  Benjamin Todd, "Want to Do Good? Here's How to Choose an Area to Focus On," 80,000 Hours, March 2017. Available from: https://80000hours.org/career-guide/most-pressing-problems/.
26  Albert Bandura, "The Psychology of Chance Encounters and Life Paths," *American Psychologist* 37, no. 7 (July 1982): 749. Available from: http://www.itari.in/categories/higherpurpose/psychology_of_life.pdf.
27  Finlo Rohrer, "The Slow Death of Purposeless Walking," *BBC News Magazine*, May 1, 2014. Available from: http://www.bbc.co.uk/news/magazine-27186709.
28  Ibid.

# PART II

# HYPERCONNECTEDNESS AND NETWORKED LIFE

# CHAPTER 4

# HYPERCONNECTEDNESS AND THE PERILS OF BEING "ON"

Several years ago, I met with a student affairs leader from a prominent American university who had just unveiled a new first-year undergraduate leadership program. The new program consisted of a first year spent in London, in which students would be exposed to a broad array of leadership activities while also taking their undergraduate courses. Not a bad setup for first-year undergraduates! I was impressed by the effort dedicated to designing this first-year course, though skeptical.

Should first-year undergraduates really spend their time thinking about cultivating so-called leadership skills? Is thinking about the cultivation of a "personal network" perhaps not what an undergraduate education is for, at least in the first year? Are there not alternative aims that should take precedence? These questions all came to mind in this meeting. Attempting some British humor, I remarked not unsarcastically that the program seemed conducive to creating "mini-executives," to which my counterpart responded—with complete sincerity—"Exactly!"

A leadership program for first-year students seemed unnecessarily professional, encouraging students to think of themselves as executives *well* before this should ever take place. Second, what struck me was my colleague's acceptance as to the need for such a program, there appearing to be little critical reflection about why an undergraduate leadership course is worth pursuing.

Beyond all of this, however, the meeting represented a much larger issue that many in their twenties and thirties struggle with in the modern world: the need to constantly be "on." That is, to always show their best selves—this reflected in the idea of becoming a mini-executive. It is the idea that we must present ourselves as polished executives in whatever we do. *Not* to partake in this game is seen as falling behind as others push forward. Nonparticipation is perceived as missing out on career opportunities.

In this chapter, I explore the work of Sherry Turkle, Andrew Sullivan and others in order to shed light on the hyperconnectedness that is now characteristic of the modern world. Together, academic sources and first-person narratives provide a sense of what hyperconnectedness is, as well as what it does to our lives without us necessarily perceiving the consequences. Further to this, I argue that the networked lives of which we are a part promote a false sense of authenticity, *even though* terms such as "vulnerability" or exhortations for individuals to be themselves pervade our public discourse. Millennials, I think, sense this discrepancy, but often feel unable (or are simply unwilling) to overcome this superficiality.

## THE PERFORMANCE OF IDENTITY

A central idea in Turkle's work is that networks promise more but ultimately offer *less*. Indeed, "in a tethered world, too much is possible, yet few can resist measuring success against a metric of what they could accomplish if they were always available."[1] We communicate in greater volume and with more frequency than ever before, and yet, this very communication is limiting. Specifically, "the self shaped in a world of rapid response measures success by calls made, e-mails answered, texts replied to, contacts reached."[2]

Thus, the goal for individuals in a hyperconnected world is to be *on*, this being necessary for us to keep up with the demands of the supposedly rapidly changing world in which we live. Turkle rightly acknowledges that hyperconnectedness leads individuals to feel as if they are "master[s] of the universe,"[3] though in reality, most are likely less productive, more confused and more anxious than they would have been without such facilities at their disposal. We are weighed down by the very opportunities presented to us.

Hyperconnectedness is not only conducive to anxiety. It is perhaps more importantly a barrier to identity formation. Turkle states that "the years of identity formation can be a time of learning what you think by hearing what you say to others."[4] But our hyperconnection brings into doubt the very quality of what we say, in addition to how others *listen*. This is because "performances of identity may feel like identity itself."[5] But "you can present yourself as you wish to be 'seen.' And you can 'process' people as quickly as you want to. Listening can only slow you down."[6]

Several of the smartest millennials whom I know have recently indicated to me that much of an activity's value is in its sharing. The sharing that they refer to does not take place through in-person conversation but rather through online sharing. What matters is not that a person went boating or that they attended some exclusive leadership trip in another country. Instead it is that they *share* parts of these experiences with their friends and colleagues. Without sharing, activities are less significant than they would otherwise be. These people are, I believe, grossly mistaken, and I will delve further into the idea of sharing and listening later on in this chapter. But for now, we can explore several other examples.

Along with Turkle's research, Sullivan's article "I Used to Be a Human Being" is among the outstanding contributions to modern discussion on hyperconnectedness. It is perhaps surprising that Sullivan too succumbs to the difficulties of networked life, given his incisiveness as a thinker and writer. His story is particularly frightening, in that he required a lengthy hiatus from the Internet in order regain his sense of normalcy in life. As a columnist, Sullivan considered himself to be "a very early adopter of what we might now call living-in-the-web," remarking in his essay that "as the years went by, I realized I was no longer alone […] More and more people got a smartphone—connecting them instantly to a deluge of febrile content, forcing them to cull and absorb and assimilate the online torrent as relentlessly as I had once."[7]

Sullivan acknowledges that at the height of his life in-the-web, it became impossible to muster the attention required to read books, various interruptions preventing him from focusing on any given task at hand. He notes that hyperconnectedness "changes us."[8] Our hyperconnectedness "slowly removes—without our even noticing it—the very spaces where we can gain a footing in our minds and souls that is not captive to constant pressures or desires or duties."[9] For Sullivan, his time spent online was a "zero-sum question," in that the hours spent connected to the Internet were hours not dedicated to in-person activities—activities in the physical world, with fellow human beings.[10]

Audiences surely matter, but excessive awareness of one's listeners can place undue attention on the presentation of the message and in turn corrupt its content. In the modern world, personal branding is seen as important because of our hyperconnectedness, in that we can showcase ourselves through multiple platforms, with the sort of volume and frequency indicated by Turkle. However, to actively build and maintain a personal brand is usually disingenuous. The rise of the personal brand runs parallel, I think, to millennials' fixation with TEDx presentations. Though shiny and appealing at first glance, when pressing further, critical thinkers begin to (hopefully!) see through these appearances, realizing that little originality lies beneath the smoke and mirrors.

## A CASE AGAINST CONSISTENT ONLINE SHARING

We can now return to the earlier comment from Part I on sharing, which I believe requires more focused examination. The argument that many thoughtful individuals put forward is that the sharing of a given activity instills in the activity a significance that would otherwise not be attained had the activity remained private (that is, where only the participants in the activity know about it). Few people, in my experience, consider what can be *lost* through the online sharing of an activity. In other words, we are now at a point where it is taken for granted that sharing is usually beneficial, if not natural. Thus, if a person accomplishes something important, then they should *of course* share it online with peers, this being an advantage in our increasingly networked lives.

Our penchant for perpetual sharing is framed as showcasing "authentic" experience. The images that we encounter online are believed to be honest, providing us with glimpses into the emotions associated with a particular endeavor. Contrary to this common interpretation, however, the desire to share actually corrupts our understanding of honesty and diminishes the significance of a given activity in an important way.

The reasoning is as follows. Seldom, in our hyperconnected world, do individuals do simply for the sake of doing good. Rather, activity is now undertaken with a view to *how it will be seen*. Something important is lost on an individual level when we do this. Our intentions, which might have originally been pure—activity aiming toward nothing else than doing good—are instrumentalized. We begin to consider the anticipated reaction to a potential activity as part of our mental calculus in taking action. This kind of thinking chips away at our integrity and diminishes our autonomy.

When we share so actively online, we imply that the material shared is worth others' time (at the very least, it is worth others' time *seeing* what is shared, even if for a second). Put slightly differently, we might even say that the sharer posts something online because they want to *know* or at least *believe* that what they share is important. In other words, one wants to feel like what they have to say matters. We seek validation and relevance.

This kind of philosophy behind sharing has multiple consequences, most of which I believe are negative, whether or not people are conscious of this. The first is that it provides individuals with a sense that what they are doing—or what they have to say— is meaningful. (This is not to say what millennials do or accomplish as a generational cohort does not *matter*—to say this would of course be wrong.) Instead, what I'm saying is that there is much that is shared that is not actually of very much significance, *even if* the person sharing material thinks otherwise. Certainly it is important that individuals are able to share their feelings and experiences in general, for dialogue provides opportunities to sharpen our thinking and learn more about ourselves. Moreover, through dialogue, specifically with wise persons, we learn how to say things more concisely, as well as how to frame our knowledge in a way that we previously did not think possible.

This sort of dialogue is important. But the kind of sharing that I'm attempting to describe is, more often than not, antithetical to this. Indeed, because of the ability to share online with such volume and frequency—elevating ordinary experience through careful editing based on the responses that we anticipate and desire—individuals begin to feel that their opinions are significant *before* they have necessarily informed themselves or have engaged in sufficient self-reflection.

The modern propensity to share allows people to fool themselves, believing that, because they receive such rapid and affirmative responses to what they say online, what they say or do is automatically of importance. This gives rise to the plethora of young activists keen to campaign for social causes, firm in their convictions, without having acquired the life experience necessary to consider why they even hold such convictions. Though independent and critical thinking are regularly espoused as much-needed modern skills, they appear to be in rather short supply.

A second point, building on the first, is that people set themselves up for frustration and disappointment in cases where they realize that their experiences are in fact less unique than they originally thought. To take the idea of the personal brand, hundreds if not thousands of millennials wiggle their way into giving TEDx talks and comparable motivational presentations. Some realize—though many, unfortunately, never do—that what they present isn't actually very original or innovative. But their talks are posted online for all to see.

We should consider whether individuals' frequency of online sharing, and the validation resulting from this, might not *entrench* opinions and thereby hinder learning and self-reflection in our relative youth. In other words, we erect for ourselves barriers to curiosity and intellectual exploration during a formative period of life. The lack of critical online discussion allows most of us to get away with ill-informed perspectives, insulating ourselves from meaningful conversation in which we can learn to engage with constructive criticism.

A further consequence of our propensity to share is that it contributes to self-comparison, a point that I will take up in Chapter 3. For now, it suffices to say that based on my observations of millennials, they begin to fear that others' experiences and reflections are more meaningful than theirs. There is now a label for this: F.O.M.O., or the "fear of missing out."

In the considerable time that millennials spend online, they look at what their friends say and do, and begin to wonder how others' experiences are so interesting and exciting. In perusing my Facebook timeline this morning, for instance, I see how one friend spent the weekend on a retreat in Switzerland, how another built for herself a "smart room" equipped with fancy raspberry pi devices, and how another is clearly enjoying his first few weeks of MBA life.

Meanwhile, I stayed primarily at home, celebrated my birthday with several calls with family and a few close friends and chose to read a book rather than organize a party. When looking at what my peers got up to, seeing photos from other friends' recent birthdays, there were several instances in which I felt tinges of loneliness. Comparison does this to us.

## FALSE AUTHENTICITY

The trouble with the modern inclination to share online is that it is often considered *authentic*. Turkle beautifully captures hyperconnectedness by saying that we often mistake the performance of identity for identity itself. If a person spends a considerable amount of time sharing photos of their travels say as a journalist, showcasing the many different parts of a country and the diverse peoples that they meet along the way, then onlookers begin to see the journalist *as* living the life they present. Unless a person knows this journalist well, and spends time in conversation face-to-face or over the phone, then it can be hard to see through the facade. Most of us, I think, are generally aware of this illusion, though— unwilling or simply unable for lack of time or energy to dig deeply into what we see in others' sharing—follow the path of least resistance, which is that of likewise curating our own digital identities.

We can think of this a bit differently, however, asking ourselves what are the consequences for individuals who do *not* engage in this sort of curated sharing. If we are to actually be ourselves, shedding the constant presentation, then what might be the implications? For the purpose of this discussion and in contrast to the kind of identity presented through online sharing, I see "being oneself" as coming to grips with *limitedness* in our selves. Having a "narrative" or "story" becomes much less important. Individuals who are themselves do not put up a guard. They acknowledge that they are inherently flawed and they embrace this.

They do not feel like they need to package their experiences so that they can be used as a means for impressing others.

Being oneself consists, in other words, partly in *not* needing to perform. While admirable, this form of existence is nowadays rare, as individuals without clear personal narratives or brands are looked upon strangely, as having less to offer to the world. I think for instance about a recent conversation with a friend in England, one of the smartest people I have ever met. Following a recent meeting in London, a colleague told him that he should develop a snappier 30-second pitch about himself—simply being a "writer" and "campaigner" was insufficient for impressing his counterparts.

In reality, the individual in question is an accomplished author and former clerk to a supreme court judge. He is a Rhodes Scholar, but you wouldn't know it, because he wouldn't tell you unless asked and he doesn't put it on his public biography. Though much more authentic than just about anyone in his self-conduct, acknowledging some uncertainty as to how best to thread together his several activities, this person's humble self-description was, to his friend, not impressive enough! To be oneself is difficult when performance is so often mistaken for reality.

So what should individuals do, given the pressures associated with our hyperconnection and the tools now at our disposal for consistent sharing of our lives? While succumbing to these pressures might be the path of least resistance, we need to think critically about how else we can act. I offer two interconnected suggestions as alternatives.

As previously stated, embracing limitedness in our lives is critical: it helps immensely, in the modern world, to acknowledge that we have flaws and that we make mistakes. Being honest with ourselves about this requires courage. The philosopher Michael Oakeshott writes about "a society or a generation which thinks what it has discovered for itself is more important than what it has inherited."[11] It is a society that believes in its originality and superiority over those of the past. Though first published in 1962, Oakeshott's words remain timely. Nowadays we strive to achieve certainty through validation of our self-expression. Likes received on Facebook or retweets on Twitter serve as temporary forms of approval, suggesting that ordinary experiences or public reflections are of actual significance. This gives us a sense of certainty in ourselves, but this certainty is ultimately misleading.

It is misleading, for it rests on faulty hearing. We are drawn toward dialogue that yields short-term validation based on what we *want* to hear, which gives us the sense that what we have to say is automatically meaningful. But as we have seen, the only genuine substitute for this is honesty, in which we embrace the uncertainty and messiness in our lives, along with the frustration that this brings.

The second point, which builds on the first, is that of the importance of in-person dialogue, particularly with friends who can share with us difficult truths. For this very brief discussion, we can turn to the philosopher John Dewey, who in *The Public and Its Problems* criticizes the utilitarian notion that "each person is naturally the best judge of his own interests, and, if left free from the influence of artificially imposed restrictions, will express his judgment in his choice of work and exchange of services and goods."[12] Rejecting this view, Dewey notes that "the idea of a natural individual in his isolation possessed of full-fledged wants, of energies to be expended according to his own volition, and of a ready-made faculty of foresight and prudent calculation is as much a fiction in psychology as the doctrine of the individual in possession of antecedent political rights is one in politics."[13]

The point that Dewey tries to make is that learning is ultimately *social*. It is through constructive dialogue that we learn about who we are, what matters to us and what we should dedicate our time and energy toward. It is a collective endeavor. Unfortunately, dialogue that takes place through online networks is a deficient form of learning, one that promises much but ultimately sets us back. Our collective embrace of shallow authenticity means that we must do even more work to discover truths in others and ourselves. We are forced to wade through more clutter. Thus, needed more than ever are friends with whom we can voice concerns, feel warmth and safety as we let down our guards and speak truthfully and respectfully when the circumstances so require.

## NOTES

1   Sherry Turkle, *Alone Together* (New York: Basic Books, 2011), 164.
2   Ibid., 166.
3   Ibid., 165.
4   Ibid., 175.
5   Ibid., 12.
6   Ibid., 207.
7   Andrew Sullivan, "I Used to Be a Human Being," *New York Magazine*, September 18, 2016. Available from: http://nymag.com/selectall/2016/09/andrew-sullivan-technology-almost-killed-me.html.

8　Ibid.

9　Ibid.

10　Ibid.

11　Ibid., 23.

12　John Dewey, *The Public and Its Problems* (Athens: Swallow Press & Ohio University Press, 1954), 91.

13　Ibid., 102.

CHAPTER 5

# IMPACT AND "HIGH-POTENTIAL" NETWORKS

If dishonesty is nowadays a prevalent issue, with self-presentation valued more than personal character, then the rise of "high-potential" networks is at least partly to blame. I will now focus on several of these networks, with my emphasis on the Global Shapers Community, a network associated with the World Economic Forum. My aim here is to provide some historical background on these networks, as well as comment on their consequences, both positive and negative, for the individuals invited to join. Throughout this analysis, I will argue that these networks, while serving as tremendous networking opportunities for members, provide individuals with a sense that they are far greater than they actually are. To my knowledge, there has been little, if any, public critical examination of networks such as Global Shapers over past years. It is my hope that this serves as a first step in generating some discussion on the topic. As a Global Shaper myself, much of the following analysis involves anecdotal, personal reflection.

## THE GLOBAL SHAPERS COMMUNITY

Networks for "high-potential" young leaders are ubiquitous: universities, nonprofits, corporations, and countless other institutions now develop leadership pathways for ambitious people, with words such as "talent," "rising star" and "emerging leader" used in order to describe the kinds of individuals sought. On the surface, these networks seem harmless, if not laudable. But there is reason for criticism of these sorts of initiatives, which are often less impactful than we might think.

Among the most prominent of these networks is Global Shapers, an initiative of the World Economic Forum, founded in 2011 by the executive chairman of the World Economic Forum, Klaus Schwab. According to its website, Global

Shapers "is a network of Hubs developed and led by young people who are exceptional in their potential, their achievements and their drive to make a contribution to their communities."[1] Members must fall between the ages of 20 and 30 at the time of nomination. At the time of writing, 419 hubs exist globally, totaling 5,819 members. Not surprisingly, the first hubs were launched in major cities such as New York, London and Los Angeles. Over time, midsized cities such as Edmonton and Atlanta have grown their own presences, along with hubs in Europe, Asia, Africa and Australia.

There is very little public writing about the Global Shapers Community. Thankfully, however, several recent publications in the *Huff Post* and *Medium* provide a sense of what the network is for. As a starting point, we can look to the September 2015 *Huff Post* article "Who Are the Global Shapers?" by Kirk-Anthony Hamilton, himself a Global Shaper. In this article, Hamilton writes, "The community was formed as a direct response to the 2010 uprisings in the Middle East, which revealed pressing matters, which needed to be addressed. Youth were disgruntled by their unrealized voice on issues shaping their future and youth have the ability to band together to force meaningful change. The conclusion—we are deserving of a seat at the table, to be apart [*sic*] of the decisions that affect our lives."[2] Hamilton then shares reflections on his experience at the 2015 Annual Curators Meeting, which convened over four hundred curators (essentially, these are chairs of city-based hubs), the "trust factor of the community," being "beyond compare, as many of us can confirm we opened up like never before and walked away with life long friends."[3]

A similarly titled article, "What Is the World Economic Forum Global Shapers Community, Really?" by Mariel Reed provides us with additional background on the network. Writing in *Medium*, Reed concedes that "no, Global Shapers isn't a shadow organization or cult. We're not Illuminati."[4] That said, Global Shapers are often invited to do "fancy things," such as interviewing Canadian prime minister Justin Trudeau at Davos. Reed writes that Global Shapers are tightly interconnected: "Our shared values of collaboration, service, social justice, and bias to action allow the community to share a high level of trust—even among members who have never met face to face."[5]

For Reed, three traits define Global Shapers: those of action, community and representation. Essentially, Global Shapers are committed to social causes, often within their professional work—though most certainly outside of it—with members sometimes developing bonds that transcend geographical boundaries. Reed gives what is on the whole a helpful explanation of the network. But there has been little *critical* analysis regarding Global Shapers or comparable networks. The articles are primarily descriptive. It is therefore my intention to provide a more critical perspective on Global Shapers and other similar networks. This will help illustrate what I mean by inauthenticity in the previous chapter and why it is difficult to live truthfully in modern life.

My own involvement in Global Shapers began in 2014, when I helped start the Edmonton hub, one of the first Canadian cities to establish a Global Shapers presence. I would soon after move to Cambridge, England, and in preparation for this realized that, strangely, no presence existed in the city despite hubs existing in London, Oxford, and Manchester. While in Cambridge, I helped gather approximately fifteen individuals who collectively founded the hub, and spent much of the year participating in Global Shapers events in London and Oxford. Along with Kirk-Anthony Hamilton and Mariel Reed, I participated in the 2015 Annual Curators Meeting in Geneva and have taken part in other gatherings with world leaders, such as with former British prime minister David Cameron.

I'm grateful for these and other experiences. For instance, upon first arriving in London, the then-curator of the London hub allowed me to crash in his spare room—a wonderfully kind gesture given that I had sat in an Iceland airport, only several hours earlier, unaware as to where I would stay in London later that day. Two weeks later, the London hub coincidentally held a large retreat on the southwest coast of Britain, which provided an opportunity to meet more than forty outstanding people, several of whom have since become close friends. As a result, my criticisms are not without recognition of the benefits afforded through participation in the network. My intention is thus to help generate a *constructive* public dialogue on these kinds of groups. I believe there is currently an appetite among many Global Shapers and millennials for this.

The 2015 Annual Curators Meeting represented much of what I believe is troublesome in Global Shapers and other comparable millennial networks. As Hamilton writes, the gathering provided an opportunity to connect with many interesting individuals. Yet, on the whole, I found the gathering lacking in meaningful content. It was, in short, a five-day networking event sprinkled with several panel conversations about social inequality, globalism, and other topics that one would expect to see discussed at Davos. For all of the supposed brainpower in the room, I was disappointed by the dearth of good conversation. We were reminded throughout the gathering that we must "shape": basically, that it is the responsibility of Global Shapers, the world's young changemakers, to create impact wherever they go. Much of this was uncomfortably self-congratulatory, especially given how little conversation took place among participants regarding what they *actually* believed to be the problems currently worth tackling in the world.

This should have been no surprise, for Global Shapers are excellent self-promoters. I can still remember one American participant, for instance, telling the Chengdu representative that the root of his social enterprise's challenges— this social enterprise having *far surpassed* much of what most of the American hubs had accomplished in their own work—was that they needed to "better market themselves." Of course, this American representative ran his own marketing company, and thus arrived at the conference with go-to answers for conversations with fellow participants. He had a prepackaged message to share.

The Annual Curators Meeting was, in short, a gathering in which self-promotion trumped in-depth conversation. In this and other Global Shapers gatherings, I find that "storytelling" tends to dominate. Global Shapers are too easily impressed by their own stories and see the gatherings as a means to share them with others. This takes place without *really* wanting to think critically about the issues that they are supposedly interested in addressing.

## ACTION, IMPACT AND ENTRANCE STANDARDS

Perhaps I am being too harsh on Global Shapers: the World Economic Forum is not, after all, a university. In other words, it is not a place where constructive criticism is core to the organizational mandate. There is some truth to this. The World Economic Forum, in my experience, focuses more on event management and content production than it does on meaningful discourse. But given that Global Shapers are expected to "shape the world," one would also hope that its 5,000-plus members engage in some form of constructive dialogue pertaining to the philosophy, ethics, morality, history and economics (among other important considerations) relevant to better understanding what lies at the root of particular modern issues.

Several important factors obstruct meaningful dialogue within these sorts of networks, and I will examine these in the space below. The first of these is that these networks focus on *action*, which is much different than focusing on dialogue. Related to this, Global Shapers and other networks emphasize the significance of *impact*: actions undertaken should bring about positive change in some locality. In other words, what matters at the end of the day is that these networks have something to show for their work. They must organize events, reach people, and post selfies and other evidence of success on social media. These sorts of things can be measured, and so they are more useful in the short term than encouraging discussion, which takes time, can be frustrating, and doesn't usually result in much that can be "accomplished" over a period of several months.

Third, when associated with well-known brands such as the World Economic Forum, a considerable number of members join due to the networks' signaling effects. This is just as we see with elite business schools, in which the value of an MBA for employers sometimes resides less in the intellectual rigor of a given program than in confirmation that applicants were clever enough to gain admission into a program in the first place. Fourth, the standards are simply so high for gaining membership into many of these networks that they inevitably attract ambitious, achievement-oriented individuals. The same kinds of people, that is, who strive to give TEDx talks and then post these on Facebook.

As I see it, the first two points affect the kinds of *conversations* that take place (or do not take place), and the second two points pertain more to the kinds of *people* whom networks such as Global Shapers attract. Based on my past experiences in these sorts of settings, ambitious millennials, no matter how well educated they might be on paper, or whatever kinds of entrepreneurial ventures they might be a part of, are not great contributors to constructive discussion. Although the networks label them as "thought leaders," many seem to gain satisfaction through the rehashing of intellectual fads. A select few are original and courageous in what they think, but this is the exception in these networks.

Taking action in the world in order to solve problems is essential, but we need more than just action. More specifically, society needs moral courage in action. In reading Thurston Clarke's *The Last Campaign*, one is struck by the emphasis that both John F. and Bobby Kennedy gave to moral rather than physical courage throughout their political careers—something that we would all benefit from reflecting on.[6] Indeed, action for the sake of action is often futile, an idea that academics John L. Elias and Sharam B. Merriam capture when they write, "theory without practice leads to an empty idealism, and action without philosophical reflection leads to mindless activism."[7] Global Shapers and other similar networks struggle to overcome this hurdle. Obsessed with action, they bypass dialogue, seeing this as a frivolous activity contrary to achieving the aim of impact.

In her *Medium* article, Reed writes, "Global Shapers take action. In our individual professional lives, many of us are dedicated to social causes. But outside our day jobs, we are Global Shapers because we choose to commit time together to collaborate on projects that improve our communities. Some Hubs initiate totally new projects and ideas; others amplify the work of outstanding nonprofit organizations."[8] Reed is correct to say that Global Shapers *are* action-oriented individuals by nature, with considerable energy and a collective desire to change the world. However, in my experience with Global Shapers, the kinds of activities that tend to take place through this action are things like "hackathons," speaker sessions and other short-term projects that ensure that hubs keep themselves occupied.

A hackathon might take place with a local nonprofit looking for technological solutions to a lingering problem. Global Shapers will then identify a dozen or so members from a particular city or region, who will spend several hours meeting with the organization in order to offer solutions. This might seem like a constructive form of dialogue, but helpful dialogue is rare. More often than not, the conversations are similar to the previous Chengdu example, in that participants come with ready-made answers.

This occurred, for instance, in the 2015 SHAPE North America conference, a continent-wide gathering of Global Shapers hosted in Edmonton and Calgary, in which a two-hour meeting took place between several dozen Global Shapers and one of Canada's premier vocational colleges. The college executives asked Global Shapers to engage on several questions pertaining to technical education, and in typical fashion, the ensuing group dialogue consisted of people talking past each other.

Shortly after I first moved to England, the very issue of "action versus dialogue" emerged at the conclusion of a Global Shapers retreat, in which forty or so individuals spent two days together, traversing the southwest coast and talking into the early hours of the morning. During a retreat debriefing session, a particularly outspoken member pushed against the idea that the London hub should spend more time organizing action-oriented events (such as hackathons) and instead view the hub as a means for generating interesting conversations between the Global Shapers *themselves*. There was a hush in the room.

At the time, I was firmly in the "action" camp, and could not fathom how a member could see the network simply as a means for discussion. However, in hindsight, this individual had a point. One of the major consequences of the action-first attitude is that the actions tend not to endure. Organized too hastily, and without sufficient support within a given hub, there is little meaningful follow-up on whatever is initially accomplished. A brainstorming session might take place with a local nonprofit, but the engagement begins and ends there.

This begs an important question. Are networks like Global Shapers really to blame for this lack of rich discussion? Certainly, they must share some responsibility, action being so central to the networks' missions. Yet, I have previously argued (in Part I) that universities have themselves become too outcomes focused. Indeed, the very institutions in which open dialogue is supposed to take place are relinquishing their responsibilities.

Seeing themselves as economic engines, bent on commercializing their research and on producing graduates ready-made for the workforce, universities conclude that adaptability is the ideal to which all graduates should aspire. If our main educational institutions fail to promote constructive dialogue, then what should we really expect of other institutions and organizations with semieducational mandates?

The workforce, entrenched in students' minds, diverts attention toward practical activities—clubs, societies and start-ups—at the expense of time spent on reading, exploration and critical reflection. Thinking activities play second fiddle to action-oriented activities. Society suffers the consequences. This shift has manifested itself over the course of many decades, but young people bear the brunt of it.

Only the most curious of individuals desire to *inform* themselves during their time in university. Most are content to simply meet the low standards required to pass, with many seeing university as a means to articulate ideas that already provide them with intellectual comfort. This mindset flows into the workforce. Universities exist within a wider culture of performance, in which productivity, competitiveness and outcomes are preeminent. But they deserve much criticism.

The second challenge with Global Shapers and other networks is that they aim to create *impact*, both locally and globally. I find this issue more troubling than that of action, which is at least admirable when undertaken with some moral conviction. The trouble with impact, as we've seen already, is that it presupposes that a person knows what matters to a particular group. There is a certain arrogance among many of those who speak publicly about creating impact, and moreover, about doing so at *scale*. In the wake of Britain's referendum vote to leave the EU, many Global Shapers wondered how they could better understand "those" who voted to leave. This sort of looking-down-upon-others attitude was even more prevalent following the election of Donald Trump as president of the United States.

There is, in short, a righteousness in which a particularly well-educated group of people believes that they know better than others what is good for them, and thus should enter their communities in order to solve their various problems (this being called impact). This is what produces hackathons and other fruitless events that disintegrate shortly after takeoff. This is not to say that many Global Shapers do not *want* to meaningfully engage with a wide range of groups or that meaningful activity along these lines does not take place. Indeed, there are some Global Shapers who do care about improving the world, and who do so quietly, without regard for recognition.

This righteousness would be more bearable were it not for many Global Shapers' propensity to share their impactful activities for all to see online. Selfies are core to the Global Shapers Community: it is a network in which the image dominates. In one particularly striking instance, a Global Shaper posted on Facebook, following a Brexit-focused gathering with David Cameron, that he had been invited to *meet* with the prime minister and was there "endorsed" by a whole slew of multinational corporations and prominent individuals. The reality is that the gathering was in fact *not* a meeting with Cameron—to write this was to stretch the truth as far as possible. Unfortunately, this sort of behavior is typical in Global Shapers and other networks.

What matters these days is not that a group creates impact, but that it is seen or believed to create impact. In thinking about these sorts of millennial networks, David Brooks's writing often comes to mind, in which he argues that fame is now its own modern virtue. So many of us desire fame, to be in the limelight and thus to feel that we are special or unique. And so I cannot help but question the intentions underlying many colleagues' impact-driven activities. Is it creating impact that matters (i.e., really helping people), or is it that appearing to create impact provides individuals with validation conducive to their desired appearances? There are of course many exceptions, but I'm generally inclined to believe the latter.

In Global Shapers, we see people who, for the most part, are thoughtful individuals. They bring to their city hubs great expertise: some are doctors, some are academics, and some are entrepreneurs, to name only a few categories. Provided with time to engage critically with each other—to share in constructive dialogue—they might learn something about their various professions, and in turn, develop more nuanced understandings of their *own* work. This was one of the main benefits of the aforementioned London retreat in 2015: in one activity, participants spent several hours gathered in a large circle, each person sharing observations from their field of work or research for three minutes. Unfortunately, though, when hubs begin to drive toward impact, their attention moves away from such discussion.

It is here that pedestrian ideas such as hackathons or speakers series are tossed around. This detracts from what could take place within these networks, if only more time was spent in conversation. Impact has gained such status in modern culture that it is unlikely that networks such as Global Shapers will veer from this framework any time soon. Universities have begun to think in the same way. Certainly, institutions require feedback mechanisms that ensure their members undertake good work. Impact addresses this concern, but it often leads us astray. Indeed, we would probably create more impact if we were *not* to aim for it. More time spent in dialogue—without a view to what this will produce— would better uncover our own flaws and limitations, and allow us to engage with others with greater patience and moderation.

But such dialogue is hard to come by when individuals often join these networks because of their signaling effects. There is much to be gained for individuals who associate themselves with prestigious brands. And in the case of the Global Shapers Community, there are few international organizations with a reputation as strong as the World Economic Forum.

As far as prestige goes, one millennial-focused event stands out from the others: the "Davos 50," an elite gathering of young leaders selected annually for the main World Economic Forum gathering in Davos, Switzerland. Participation in Davos as one of the Davos 50 is considered a significant honor, providing the opportunity to rub shoulders with the likes of Bill Clinton, Christine Lagarde and Justin Trudeau.

When it comes to social media, it is difficult for a millennial to find much better material for peer validation. Thus, every January, my Facebook timeline lights up with images of the Davos 50 celebrating, interviewing world leaders such as Trudeau, and taking in the sights and scenery of the small Swiss ski town. The Global Shapers brand and these exclusive gatherings appeal to the sense of belonging that each of us desires. Prior to helping start the Edmonton hub, for instance, I remember feeling a tinge of jealously toward a Torontonian friend that had just recently joined the newly established Toronto hub. Certainly, the network itself seemed interesting, but it was the brand that I found most compelling.

If the brand is the basis for associating with a particular activity, then this limits constructive dialogue from the very outset. For individuals seeking meaningful dialogue, this creates a near-insurmountable challenge. One of the main problems that Global Shapers (and the many other networks associated with well-known brands) face is that members simply do not engage after being accepted. Several of the more clever hubs implement probationary periods, say for three to six months, for this very reason.

This ensures that individuals do not receive the benefit of a "badge" without contributing meaningfully to a project—or at least showing up to meetings. Probationary periods aside, however, my point is that the reasons for an organization's existence (in other words, what an organization is ultimately *for*), and the structure developed to reflect this philosophy, significantly influence the kinds—and quality—of activities that it organizes. Badge collecting is tempting, but there is a point at which there are diminishing returns. It is better for a person to realize this sooner rather than later in life.

This is because badge collecting, though impressive on the surface, does not require much effort. Once one has entered the virtuous cycle of networks, new opportunities to engage in other networks present themselves rather consistently.

But the reality is that there are tradeoffs between sales and the cultivation of one's "intellectual capital." In short, as one spends more time in "hustling" mode, fewer hours can be spent in self-reflection, reading and engaging with others in meaningful conversation. The kind of sales required for participation in many of these networks is antithetical to curiosity and introspection. And the quality of networks suffers accordingly.

## NETWORKS AND THEIR CONSEQUENCES

Global Shapers is of course far from the only reputable millennial community or network. In addition to this, the *Forbes* Under 30 list annually showcases "600 of the brightest young entrepreneurs, innovators and game changers" across the world.[9] Given the magazine's brand, the Under 30 list has significant clout among individuals in their twenties and thirties and a geographical reach stretching across the world (lists are created for North America, Europe, Africa and Asia). Sandbox, NEXUS, Hive, and Singularity University also run their own networks and communities.

In addition to the above networks, corporations have themselves begun to develop networks for "high-potential" young people. Some are simply referred to as "leadership programs," others as "emerging leaders programs" and then others as "futures programs." These exist within a plethora of corporations: Boeing, Northrop Grunman, Ford, The Kraft Heinz Company, Unilever, GE, Siemens, GlaxoSmithKline, and so on— the list is endless.[10] Indeed, these kinds of networks are now quite common.

Even *universities* now have selective leadership programs for their students. My alma mater, the University of Alberta, is a case in point, recently calling upon former Canadian Prime Minister Kim Campbell to help launch the Peter Lougheed Leadership College, which is dedicating at least $70 million to the development of programs and physical facilities for ambitious midyear undergraduates. The program identifies approximately one hundred students per year from across disciplines; brings them together through common living spaces, leadership courses and extracurricular activities; and intends to send graduates into other programs (such as the Rhodes Scholarship or the recently launched Schwarzman Scholarship).

These networks share many commonalities. First, each strives to attract "rising stars" or "emerging leaders"—a claim that I will dissect shortly. Second, these networks fancy themselves as spaces in which members can be vulnerable, opening up with each other in ways that are difficult even with their own family members. And third, they provide members with prestige. I will conclude this chapter by briefly addressing each of these claims. However, prior to doing so, it is worth discussing *why* it is that such networks have been established over the last decade (these networks are, after all, relatively new—Global Shapers launched for instance only in 2011).

A major reason for the sprouting of these networks is that of competitiveness. Given the "war for talent" in modern work, employers feel that they must develop more attractive opportunities for potential recruits, and so they establish leadership programs. On the "buyer" side, feeling considerable pressure to distinguish themselves from their peers, millennials search for credentials that sit *outside* of traditional forms of education, through networks such as Global Shapers. These networks provide members with opportunities to "self-actualize," that is, to supposedly better understand their values through conversations and experiences with like-minded peers. And finally, these networks are often borne out of distrust in long-standing institutions, individuals feeling that they must create new initiatives in order to bring about the change that they wish to see in the world. We have addressed each of these points, to varying degrees, in Part I, but I will now return to these themes as they apply to networks.

McKinsey, in 1997, developed the now-popular idea of the "war for talent." Twenty years later, the word "talent" remains with us, firmly entrenched in our culture. Whether in publications such as the *Harvard Business Review*, *Fortune* or *Fast Company*, the word "talent" is front and center. In a world that is seen as increasingly competitive and fast moving, in which young people search for the best possible opportunities and "vote with their feet," employers bend over backward in order to attract those assumed to be the best and the brightest.

There are certainly critiques of this idea, Malcolm Gladwell being one of these. Gladwell takes aim at one of the blue-chip companies highlighted in the book *The War for Talent* (written by McKinsey staff) for its supposed talent management prowess—Enron—asking, "what if Enron failed not in spite of its talent mindset but because of it? What if smart people are overrated?"[11]

Gladwell is correct in his questioning of the talent myth, but the myth persists nonetheless. Employers worry about not attracting the best talent, and so form millennial leadership networks in order to address this. My experience working alongside employers in a wide range of industries suggests that leadership networks tend to be rather piecemeal and ineffective. They set high expectations for entrants and then usually fail to deliver. But for employers, the value of these networks lies primarily in the marketing value, in that the networks *suggest* to potential recruits that a company cares about developing its emerging leaders (and that there is a clear path to leadership for them).

For young professionals, the idea of the "war for talent" is more damaging than it is for employers. Though they do not necessarily speak in terms of a *war* for talent, young people are acutely aware that they must compete against hundreds if not thousands of their peers—many of whom are ambitious and highly skilled—for a limited number of spaces in the workforce. As a result, they search for whatever opportunities can set them apart, with emerging leaders networks chief among these. In the UK civil service, the "Fast Stream" for instance attracted applications from over 20,000 graduates for approximately 900 roles, as noted by *The Guardian*.[12]

Programs like the Fast Stream emphasize that they serve as fast tracks to leadership. This is not necessarily the case, as one can progress into leadership through a myriad of pathways, though few individuals in the formative stages of their careers are aware of this, or confident enough in themselves to resist these networks. They feel great pressure to apply and believe that an unsuccessful application severely dents their career prospects. Many individuals, intensely focused on advancing their careers, believe that to fail in these early applications will spell doom for much of the rest of their lives.

In a world that glorifies entrepreneurship, people often launch their own initiatives, rather than spend time within existing structures where change comes about much more slowly. Working with people whom we do not like, or with whom we do not share values, invites disagreement. This disagreement can conveniently be avoided through the launch of new initiatives. This, I think, is the sort of mindset that underlies many millennial leadership networks. It is a mindset that frowns upon or rejects tradition and that glorifies the new. It is an approach that places "values" at the center of activity. If we are to ask, however, about *which* values are to be prioritized, these are in most cases the values of the individual, divorced from—or framed without consideration or appreciation for—those with which the individual does not agree.

Having noted why I believe millennial networks have gathered such momentum in recent years, I will now address and critically examine several of their major claims. Among the major claims is that these networks are home to "high potential leaders." That is, the world's future chief executives, academics, politicians, activists and so forth. But what does it really mean to be a high-potential leader? This idea is rarely critically examined, which is unfortunate, because once examined we begin to see that it is tenuous. My experience contributing to these networks is that they often appeal to the most ambitious of millennials, those with lengthy curricula vitae and with impressive educational credentials. But these things do not necessarily suggest potential.

Usually, these individuals tend to have had privileged upbringings and are by and large white. Some networks and hubs are more conscious of diversity than others. In Cambridge, for instance, our initial Global Shapers hub was able to reorient itself after realizing that the first four individuals recruited to the hub were white males. But generally, diversity is a problem. This is compounded by the fact that many of the high-potentials are really just individuals who shamelessly market themselves: people with well-crafted personal narratives. Those who have their heads down and who invest *time* in a particular craft, at the expense perhaps of extracurricular activities such as leadership networks, do not usually qualify for this high-potential label.

Time will tell whether the individuals involved in these networks actually move on to positions of leadership in their respective fields. For the time being, however, badges such as Global Shapers provide individuals with a cushion of sorts in their various pursuits. As one colleague involved in these networks tells me, they "insulate the position of the already successful." The individuals who have their heads down, and who do not seek opportunities for self-promotion, might in fact be (and probably are!) more capable than their peers. In other words, they might be more intelligent, more thoughtful, and just as, if not more, hardworking. But these sorts of people are often hesitant to put themselves out there, asking, "Why me?"

Really, this seems to be the Dunning-Kruger effect at work, in which individuals with low ability, lacking self-awareness, tend to believe themselves to be greater than they are. (Conversely, the most capable individuals tend to think less of themselves, for they more clearly understand the limits of their knowledge or ability.) The risk in these leadership networks is that they, in appealing to the most confident and ambitious of people, become playgrounds for the average. As far as I can see, the only remedy to this is that leaders within these networks think about these risks and recruit "talent" accordingly.

Second, millennial networks emphasize the importance of vulnerability between members. As a participant in one of these networks once told me, "Vulnerability is a transformative superpower that empowers everyone around you to be themselves." But vulnerability too often becomes its own performance. In far too many leadership retreats, for instance, individuals will sit in a circle, each person asked to share a personal story. The aim is to entice participants to share information of an ever-deeper and more revealing quality as time progresses. This in turn encourages the comparatively hesitant participants to do the same. Many participants understand this game and become adept at sharing information that is *just vulnerable enough*, ensuring that what they say elicits the intended responses from colleagues.

We see in many of these networks a false authenticity, in which individuals portray themselves as they wish to be seen. Many are fooled into believing that such performances are real, that they reflect individuals as they really *are*, which probably helps explain the explosion in the self-help industry over past years. There are countless "executive coaches" out there willing to help the high-potentials of the world *find themselves* through a sort of forced vulnerability in conversation. (When approached by these coaches, the best response is usually to just walk, or run, away.) Vulnerability cannot be forced. It is the result of a slow building of trust between individuals. There is little to gain—though perhaps much to lose—by interrupting this process.

Indeed, these networks provide members with titles, but require little responsibility. Participants say that they desire to change the world, but few reflect on what changes are most worth pursuing or why change is even needed in the first place. The prestige associated with titles such as Global Shapers allows the most ambitious of Global Shapers to travel from one city to the next, building tremendous personal networks for themselves. But the foundation upon which these networks are built is fragile. Projects and relationships are thus short-lived. Once having gained entry to the networks, these ambitious individuals have all that they need: a currency to be exchanged for entry into other clubs and societies.

I have in this chapter attempted to explain some of the reasons behind the emergence of millennial networks, while also commenting on their consequences. Global Shapers, being one of the more prominent international networks, and the one with which I'm most familiar, is the primary object of attention. In describing Global Shapers and comparable networks, I identify several commonalities among them: their focus on attracting those considered to be of "high potential," the central role of vulnerability in the members' proceedings, and the prestige associated with membership.

Given the surprising lack of critical examination into these networks over the last several years, I have sought to address some of their main features, with the intention of generating a wider discussion among participants as to the networks' merits. My driving point in this criticism of networks is that they are often severely lacking in the realm of *dialogue*. I do want to make clear that these networks do attract some outstanding people of real character. Yet, there is little of enduring intellectual or social value that emerges from most of these kinds of initiatives. The result is that these networks, despite claiming to attract high-potentials, do not *themselves* live up to their potential.

## NOTES

1  The Global Shapers Community, "Introducing the Global Shapers Community." Available from: https://www.globalshapers.org/about-us-0.

2  Kirk-Anthony Hamilton, "Who Are the Global Shapers?" *Huff Post*, September 3, 2015. Available from: http://www.huffingtonpost.com/kirkanthony-hamilton/who-are-the-global-shaper_b_8068440.html.

3  Ibid.

4  Mariel Reed, "What Is the World Economic Forum Global Shapers Community, Really?" *Medium*, July 30, 2017. Available from: https://medium.com/world-economic-forum-global-shapers-san-francisco/what-is-the-world-economic-forum-global-shapers-community-really-42c96eb7386f.

5  Ibid.

6  Thurston Clarke, *The Last Campaign* (New York: Henry Holt and Company, 2008).

7  John Elias and Sharan Merriam, *Philosophical Foundations of Adult Education* (Malabar: Krieger Publishing, 2004).

8  Reed, "What Is the World Economic Forum Global Shapers Community, Really?"

9  Caroline Howard and Emily Inverso, "Forbes 30 Under 30," January 3, 2017. Available from: https://www.forbes.com/30-under-30-2016/#71cd017b3afb.

10  Columbia University Center for Career Education, "Leadership Development & Rotational Programs," 2018. Available from: https://www.careereducation.columbia.edu/resources/leadership-development-rotational-programs.

11  Malcolm Gladwell, "The Talent Myth," *New Yorker*, July 22, 2002. Available from: http://www.newyorker.com/magazine/2002/07/22/the-talent-myth.

12  Tamsin Rutter, "How to Join the Civil Service Fast Stream," *The Guardian*, September 1, 2015. Available from: https://www.theguardian.com/public-leaders-network/2014/sep/01/civil-service-fast-stream-how-to-join-graduate-careers.

# CHAPTER 6

# COMPARISON, SUCCESS STORIES AND LISTS

Not all millennials will join the types of networks described in the previous chapter, but the majority spends much of its time online and, thus, is sucked into a world of comparison with others. Comparison is a problem for this generation. It is persistent—difficult to escape in our digital universe—and takes place in multiple ways. Access to constant opportunities for comparison creates a belief that success comes quickly, and that we can achieve our goals by understanding how others have achieved theirs.

Expectation of rapid progress is the source of considerable anxiety among today's young people and is heightened by the idea that age is of little significance in modern life. Worried that we are not doing enough in the early stages of our working lives—though also in the developmental stage of emerging adulthood—we arrive at a crossroads. My aim in this chapter is to critically examine the nature of comparison in modern life, after which we can move to an analysis of solitude, in Part III.

## RUTHLESS COMPARISON

As part of a client project in 2016, I spent much of the year interviewing students, graduates and employers in science fields in order to better understand what it meant to them to be a scientist or, at the very least, a student of science. The client was a science faculty in a major North American public research university. Its deanery had grown concerned in past years about science undergraduates who did not adequately reflect on why they pursued science degrees. Many of the students viewed science as a means toward practicing medicine, science degrees being the usual entryway to medical school at Canadian universities.

Over time, it became apparent that interviewees struggled with comparison, rarely feeling like their achievements were ever enough. Comparison served as a barrier to contemplation and self-reflection, these kinds of activities seen as antithetical to progress—especially when friends and colleagues appeared to race forward in their lives. One particularly insightful interviewee described the problem as follows:

> My first intuition is to blame it [comparison] on the stories we are told, of the people that we admire […] We are a generation that is ruthlessly comparing ourselves with those around us and our role models at the same time. And if we are not doing something exceptional or feel important and fulfilled for what we are doing […] then we have a hard time. At least with what I've seen of people, we have a very hard time praising or being very happy.

I find this is a generation that, believing the world to be more competitive than ever, spends copious amounts of time thinking about what their peers are doing with their lives. Faced with a myriad of choices as to what they can do with their lives, they direct their attention outside of themselves and so struggle mightily with assumptions as to how others' lives unfold.

It is worth beginning with a brief discussion on the psychology of comparison, which suggests that comparison with others contributes to negative self-affect and a decrease in beliefs of self-efficacy. A first glimpse into the consequences resulting from comparison can be found in the work of psychologists Albert Bandura and Forest J. Jourden. In their 1991 paper "Self-Regulatory Mechanisms Governing the Impact of Social Comparison on Complex Decision Making," the authors attempt to better understand how comparison between one's own performance and the performance of colleagues affects self-efficacy beliefs. Bandura, one of the preeminent psychologists of his generation and a pioneer of social learning theory, defines self-efficacy as one's belief in one's ability to complete particular tasks.

Individuals with high self-efficacy believe they are capable of bringing about intended change in the world. Those with low self-efficacy demonstrate less confidence in what they can accomplish through their actions. Bandura and Jourden remark that prior to this 1991 study, most of the research on comparison focused on *why* individuals compare themselves with others. Little if any research to their knowledge had to that point investigated the effects of comparison on self-efficacy beliefs.

In this study, Bandura and Jourden selected 60 participants, all business students, and tasked them with overseeing 10 employees in a simulated, online game. The business students served as managers in a complex business and were asked to "match employee attributes to subfunctions and […] master a complex set of decision rules on how best to guide and motivate their supervisees."[1] The 60 participants took part in several rounds of employee matching, with feedback provided at the conclusion of each round. When provided with feedback, the participants' achievements were compared against a peer benchmark, allowing them to undertake self-evaluation with their colleagues' successes in mind. For the benchmark-based feedback, the participants were divided into four categories: similar capabilities, superior capabilities, progressive mastery and progressive decline.

In some cases, the peer benchmark would improve in comparison to one's own performance, decrease in comparison or stay the same. The participants whose scores worsened in comparison to the peer benchmark over successive rounds experienced decreases in self-efficacy beliefs. Participants whose scores improved against the peer benchmark saw their self-efficacy beliefs improve. As Bandura and Jourden remarked, "Those who experienced progressive decline in their comparative status were more prone to a self-referent focus on their inability to do their job."[2] Fascinatingly, self-efficacy beliefs weakened *even when one's absolute performance improved*. Participants directed their attention to the peer benchmark rather than to their own performance. Over time, the perceived gap between self and other negatively impacted performance.

This makes sense. More often than not, when comparing ourselves with others who *appear*—at least on the surface—to be doing better in a particular domain, we feel worse about ourselves. Conversely, when comparing ourselves with individuals who seem worse off, this provides us with perspective—that perhaps, after all, our lives are not quite as difficult as they seem. In some cases, "upward comparison" might lead individuals to work harder in order to achieve a particular goal. An individual who appears to be in a superior position, or who comes across as being more skilled, can serve as a source of inspiration. In other cases, it could be that a person's competitiveness leads them to work harder in order to catch up and eventually overcome the object of comparison.

Fascinated by the work of Bandura, and with a common link in our backgrounds— Bandura, too, was born and raised in Alberta—I sent him an e-mail in late 2014 asking whether it would be possible to meet in person. One of the leading psychologists of his generation, and the author of a paper called "The Psychology of Chance Encounters and Life Paths" that significantly influenced my early life, I inquired as to whether we could meet while on a trip of mine to California. He agreed, and in a lengthy discussion about his work, offered several additional insights into the nature of comparison. Bandura remarked that comparison takes place across three dimensions: that of *self, other* and *time*. In the first of these frames, we compare performance against our own standards; in the second against actual or perceived performance in others; and in the third against past performance or future expectations.

The comparisons that I have so far discussed in this chapter are primarily that of other and time. In the Bandura and Jourden study, the 60 business participants compare themselves against the peer benchmark, which changes over time. At first, it might not be that a decrease in relative performance affects participants' self-efficacy beliefs, though over *time*, participants begin to feel that they truly are falling behind their cohort. As we see in this study, a focus on others takes us away from comparison against our *own* absolute performance over time.

We can see how none of these dimensions operates in isolation of the others. Once made explicit, we are given the language to think deliberately about which of the dimensions are most worth considering when we individually undertake self-evaluation. If focused on temporal (time) comparison, then we might realize that our self-efficacy beliefs can change based on how we think of the past or future. If we are ambitious in our life plans, then we might compare ourselves against lofty expectations. Even if we achieve much of what we set out to do, we might feel poorly about ourselves when a gap exists between achievement and expected performance. Similarly, our interpretation of history will affect self-evaluation in the present: whether the past was successful, challenging, joyous, agonizing or whatever descriptors we use will shape how we think about ourselves and thus have tangible effects on our life trajectories.

It is possible that when conservative in our future expectations, we might feel better about ourselves over time, having surpassed what we originally set out to do. This brings to mind Andrew Hill's reflections in the *Financial Times*, in which journalists who stay in the industry seem to be those with modest expectations of themselves. The challenge of comparison, as I see it, is tied in large part to the issue of authenticity (or the lack thereof), as well as to the time horizons that frame our decisions. A lack of authenticity in the world, especially with millennials, makes it difficult to set reasonable expectations for ourselves. And the speed at which the world moves raises expectations as to how quickly expectations will be achieved. This is a problematic combination for this generation, one that brings considerable anxiety.

## BEST-OF MILLENNIAL LISTS

Having discussed comparison in brief, I will shed light on several contemporary phenomena that, as vehicles for comparison, can be either inspiring or insidious. The first of these is that of "best-of" lists, of which there are nowadays many. If there is one indication of these lists' prevalence in modern culture, it might just be the article "A Selection of the 30 Most Disappointing under 30" published in the *New Yorker*. Poking fun at the *Forbes* Under 30 list, the author features a number of young people hilariously underperforming in their lives.

The list includes individuals such as Will Heller, age 26, who "After a month at a Zen silent-meditation retreat […] went back to his job at Goldman Sachs as a commodities trader in oil and gas," and Tim Harris, age 27, who "started a Bay Area summer camp where exhausted tech bros can 'unplug' for two thousand dollars a weekend."[3] My favorite profile is that of Rebecca Meyer, age 29, who "since earning her M.F.A. in fiction from Columbia […] has been at work writing her début novel in her sprawling Chinatown loft, which was paid for in full by her parents. She has written sixteen pages, and they're not very good."[4]

The above descriptions are amusing because they describe individuals who have not only failed to achieve some lofty benchmark for under-thirty success, but have failed *spectacularly* in their efforts. The writer's descriptions are antithetical to the lists highlighted in *Forbes* and other publications, in which the people showcased appear capable of doing *everything*: training for the Olympics (or at the very least running Ironman triathlons), founding and selling tech companies, writing books, climbing mountains, winning Pulitzers and completing PhDs— all seemingly at the same time.

These lists garner significant attention among millennials—and there is perhaps no better example than the annual *Forbes* Under 30 list. Commenting on the *Forbes* Under 30 members' ambition and impatience, a *Forbes* writer remarks that "their ambitions are way bigger—and perfectly suited to the dynamic, entrepreneurial and impatient digital world they grew up in."[5]

The annual lists are impressive. The 600 individuals featured in 2017 explore space, run successful start-ups, lead major educational initiatives and teach at top universities. *Forbes* notes that over fifteen thousand applications were received for the 600 slots, which translates to an entry requirement more rigorous than selection for universities such as Harvard and Stanford. No millennial list is as comprehensive as that of *Forbes*, nor does any other organization build an industry around its members with comparable scale. *Forbes* annually hosts, for instance, a summit for its five thousand-plus alumni in Jerusalem and Tel Aviv.

The *Forbes* list is daunting indeed, showcasing many of the world's likely future leaders.

But is this necessarily the case? Are these society's future leaders? It is easy to read such lists and believe that those featured are the gold standard in a particular sector or field. Worse, many readers, under the age of 30, will read these lists and feel inadequate for not yet having achieved such success in their lives—and so will seek to develop curricula vitae conducive to potentially being themselves selected in the future. Others, over the age of 30, might read such lists and wonder how they have not yet accomplished as much as a person 10 years their junior. While *Forbes* and other lists serve a useful social function in recognizing the efforts of impressive young people around the world—showing what individuals are capable of in the early parts of their lives—they simultaneously serve as material for comparison, which is usually more harmful than it is good.

The comparisons that we make are often based on incomplete information. As a result, it is possible for individuals to feel worse about themselves than their actual situations should dictate. The *Forbes* profiles are short, two or three sentences per person, and it is often difficult to get a sense as to what a person *actually* does. There are, of course, individuals on these lists whom we know well (Stephen Curry and LeBron James, for instance), but most work in a wide variety of fields unknown to us. It is difficult to see what others actually do— whether their work is substantive. The information at our disposal for comparison is limited at best.

More importantly, best-of lists are problematic in that they take readers *away* from themselves. Lists drive other-comparison, in which the standard for self-evaluation is based on what we perceive others as doing. The majority of individuals are bound in these situations to see themselves as inadequate. This is the expected result of spending time on websites in which every person featured appears to be changing the world. It follows that individuals will begin to question their own life paths, wondering how they have not accomplished nearly as much as their peers.

Comparisons between self and other set readers up for frustration and sadness. Creating unrealistic images of achievement, these lists sap energy. They actually deflate readers more than they inspire. There are, of course, exceptions: some people aspire to be featured on these lists and so will work even harder in order to achieve this. But my observations over past years suggest that there are few such cases. Rankings and lists are deeply embedded in modern culture, but we need to seriously consider what value these really add to our lives.

Millennial lists are, like the networks discussed in the previous chapter, common in our society. Countless local publications now feature their most inspiring leaders under 30 or 40 years of age. The *Boston Business Journal* runs an annual 40 Under 40 list. *Brooklyn Magazine* publishes an annual 30 Under 30 list. *Management Today*, a leading British business publication, highlights every year the Top 35 Women Under 35. *Corporate Knights*, a prominent Canadian sustainability magazine, features a Top 30 Under 30 every year. Closer to home, *Avenue Edmonton* and *Avenue Calgary* both feature their annual Top 40 Under 40.

Best-of lists will continue to be published because they help newspapers and magazines increase their readership. They draw young readers to their pages, especially through the networks of individuals selected for the lists. The newspapers and magazines that establish these sorts of lists in a particular industry position themselves as "thought leaders." Moreover, the application process serves as a meeting point with young people, with whom relationships can provide novel ideas and partnerships for the publications themselves.

These lists allow their featured members to share without appearing to be arrogant. When these lists go live, recipients can head to their Facebook and Twitter profiles, sharing the posts along with messages such as "Honored to have been recognized for such and such." This is known as the "humble brag." Validation, taking place through a third party, allows recipients to share about themselves without appearing too boastful.

Once featured in one or several lists, it becomes easier for individuals to be selected for others without necessarily even submitting applications for new lists. This provides an advantage for the individuals selected to lists at early ages, for instance even *before* turning 20 (many lists recognizing teenagers' achievements have emerged over past years). Plan International, a large international development agency, releases for example an annual Top 20 Under 20 list. Many of my Canadian friends, selected for this list as teenagers, leveraged this for newspaper op-eds and entrance into Global Shapers and other networks. As publications search for additional ideas that can help them garner younger readership, one wonders when the "Top 10 Under 10" or "Top 5 Under 5" will eventually find their way onto newspaper stands and Facebook timelines. And given the competitiveness for entrance into prestigious universities and high schools, and the resulting need for individuals to more effectively showcase their abilities, there would doubtless be a market for these.

As absurd as a Top 10 Under 10 list might be, it is also conceivable because of the power of the written word. When published, these lists become authoritative. Few question the methodology behind the selection of candidates. On the one hand, millennial lists are the *result* of a modern world in which a premium is placed on competitiveness, self-presentation and personal narrative. On the other, these lists cement these ideas. It is difficult indeed to realize that these lists are often less comprehensive than appearance suggests. If readers understood this, they would decrease the likelihood that comparisons would be made based on incomplete—and often, misleading—information. This in turn would probably lessen, even if by a small margin, our society's persistent anxiousness.

## TRADITIONS

Our anxiety results from, and contributes to, an often-comparitive search outside of ourselves for meaning. Without a moral vocabulary conducive to framing life journeys, individuals find that the search within does not reveal what they are looking for. Their personal experiences are interesting but not enough. Part of the challenge lies in considering what ends are worth pursuing in the first place. John Maynard Keynes, both an illustrious economist *and* a philosopher, believed that the practice of economics should help individuals to live "wisely, agreeably, and well."[6] His leading biographer, Robert Skidelsky, writes, "As the economy became steadily more productive he [Keynes] antici-pated a progressive reduction in the hours of work, creating the conditions for people to live 'wisely, agreeably, and well.' This was his answer to the question 'what was economics for'?"[7]

But such questions are out of fashion nowadays, considered elitist by some, patriarchal by others and then futile or retrograde by proponents of pluralism. "There are multiple possible ends, and it is up to individuals to figure these out for themselves" is the sort of response we hear nowadays. But Keynes and the Skidelskys make a very good point. Without much, if any, public dialogue regarding the kinds of things that are worth valuing in life, how are individuals to think about what their journeys are for in the first place? Without any such conversation, millennials look to others—most equally unsure about these questions—to find answers.

The implications are clear. What results is a shallow comparative thinking, reflective of John Stuart Mill's saying "Men do not desire to be rich, but to be richer than other men." Translated in modern terms, individuals give tacit assent to lists and other such publications, with the belief that they might find what they are looking for in their peers' success stories. Of course, these comparisons are always incomplete, thus leaving readers in search for more, though it is profoundly difficult to grasp what this *more* entails. This kind of search begins and ends with uncertainty and anxiety.

If the search purely within oneself fails to provide us with the meaning we desire, then to what, or to whom, should we pay attention in our journeys? What is it, in other words, that can provide us with grounding in our pursuits? What ends should frame human activity? The educational philosopher Ronald Barnett highlights the difficulty in answering this question. Barnett argues that in the modern world, the frameworks that individuals use in order to make sense of the world are *themselves* contested, resulting in the experience of "anxiety," "fragility," and "chaos." We experience a "destabilization that arises from a personal sense that we never can come into a stable relationship with the world."[8]

The fragility that individuals nowadays experience is material and psychological. But it is also spiritual. There is little doubt that people search for grounding in their lives: some sort of tradition, framework or system that provides coherence and stability in a confusing world. But we question which, if any, of these things larger than ourselves is worth embracing. Such is the challenge in a plural society. When exploring particular traditions or systems — say Catholicism or Judaism, for instance—millennials put up their defenses, fearing these kinds of serious commitments.

I think this is the case for several reasons. First, traditions are authoritative. Wisdom within traditions is greater than what individuals can discover on their own, no matter how clever they might be. But authority is today perceived negatively, as it appears to limit individual autonomy. Second, millennials tend to see traditions as being static, unchanging. This does not align with the imagined pace of modern life, where individuals must always be doing things. Third, it takes time to enter into a tradition. Such patience is rare in our society. Fourth, traditions speak to what is involved in living a good life: they refer, in other words, to worthwhile *ends*. The prominence of the individual in society makes it such that public discourse about ends, which transcend the individual, requires a lot of hard work and courage to bring to fruition.

While individuals might acknowledge that their journeys are deficient in something important—something that they cannot quite put their finger on— they would rather continue on with them than risk limiting their imagined growth through the embrace of a tradition. After all, to embrace one tradition means that doors to others close. If a person is to, say, convert to one faith, then they cannot consider becoming part of another (at least in the short term). In the modern world, closing doors is viewed negatively, for this seems to diminish the possibility for unrestrained personal growth. As discussed in Part I, it feels better to have one foot in and one foot out than to take the plunge fully into any given activity. One must always have options available.

Additionally, to embrace a tradition means that individuals must acknowledge that there are things that they do not know, and that answers to what is not known cannot always be found independently. I'm not convinced, given my previous observations of millennials, that they understand that wisdom involves dialogue with their elders and with broader traditions. Given their hyperconnectedness and the constant availability of fast answers, millennials feel that meaning can be acquired at a distance, easily and cheaply. To think about time and the worthwhile ends of an activity (that is, what activities are *for*), implies that individuals might be slowed down, and thus, that they will lose their competitive advantages in the world.

## CONCLUSION

Due to these and other factors, many people do not know where to turn. The seemingly endless options available to them in the pursuit of a purposeful life bring anxiety. Though some frameworks are appealing, each can be contested. Even if a person *were* to fully embrace one of them, other options would always exist, each making their own legitimate claims. As the psychoanalyst Adam Phillips writes, living in a world of affluence means that individuals are perpetually aware of the lives that they *could* lead, if only they wanted to.

Making commitments forces us to say no to particular options. Millennials fight against this, persuading themselves that commitments are and should be light and that it is possible—perhaps even likely—that they will pursue new things at some later date. We see this with jobs, romantic relationships and educational credentials, to name just a few examples. Careful self-reflection becomes less important when commitments are seen as being fairly trivial. After all, if commitments can be broken—the grass always being greener elsewhere— then one must not concern oneself *too much* with responsibilities in the present.

Millennials can get by with this approach. With this mentality, they needn't think for themselves about what is of real significance in their lives. Given their connectedness to various networks, there is no shortage of advice to which individuals can refer in the making of important decisions. Others can do the thinking for them. And given the rapidly changing nature of the world, individuals can justify such lightheartedness through the sense of freedom that this approach seems to offer.

To be serious about something, whether a person, a job or a decision, is looked upon more unfavorably than lightness of spirit. To be serious in the modern world is considered strange, a disadvantage, a risk when the commitments around us are liquid, to borrow the term of the late sociologist Zygmunt Bauman. To be lighthearted, however, is to ensure that one never has to think *too* hard about what one does or about what matters in life. This leaves us wanting, constantly falling short.

It is possible, in a hyperconnected world, to *appear* to succeed—say, through the acquisition of educational credentials and careful self-presentation—without needing to think for oneself. As Turkle writes, the performance of identity is often mistaken for identity itself. In modern life, one can look at what *others* do, and mistakenly believe that these kinds of lives are worth emulating. Best-of lists and networks, such as the *Forbes* Under 30 list and Global Shapers, pull readers away from themselves, providing validation where validation is not necessarily due. This focus on the other means that less time is required for thinking about one's self as a part of a larger community. That is, it becomes less important to consider simple but profoundly difficult questions: "What really matters to *me*?"; "Why do *I* really want to do this?"; "What do I *actually* think about this issue?"

In the modern world, it is possible to deceive others with this approach, floating from one thing to another while gaining recognition along the way. In doing this, it is impossible for individuals to ever know who they really *are*. The theologian Rowan Williams states, "unreality, our self-protecting illusions, our struggles for cheap security, block the way to our answering the call to be."[9] Indeed, it is possible for this generation to get away with cheap security. I argue in Parts I and II that the modern world constructs barriers to a clear understanding of self, in which individuals provide truthful responses to questions about the kinds of lives most worth leading. In Part III, I will argue that solitude is paramount in helping millennials overcome the cheap security inherent in modern life.

## NOTES

1   Albert Bandura and Forest Jourden, "Self-Regulatory Mechanisms Governing the Impact of Social Comparison on Complex Decision Making," *Journal of Personality and Social Psychology* 60, no. 6 (1991): 994. Available from: https://www.uky.edu/~eushe2/Bandura/Bandura1991JPSP.pdf.

2   Ibid., 948.

3   Bess Kalb, "A Selection of the 30 Most Disappointing Under 30," *New Yorker*, January 5, 2017. Available from: http://www.newyorker.com/humor/daily-shouts/a-selection-of-the-30-most-disappointing-under-30.

4   Ibid.

5   Ibid.

6   Robert Skidelsky, *Keynes: The Return of the Master* (London: Penguin Books, 2009), 55.

7   Ibid., 55.

8   Ronald Barnett, "Learning for an Unknown Future," *Higher Education Research & Development* 23, no. 3 (August 2004): 249–50. Available from: https://www.hv.se/globalassets/dokument/stodja/paper-theme-2–5.pdf.

9   Rowan Williams, *Open to Judgement: Sermons and Addresses* (London: Darton, Longman and Todd, 1994), 175.

# PART III

# SOLITUDE, ALONENESS
# AND LONELINESS

# CHAPTER 7

# LONELINESS AND ALONENESS

Few books in recent memory more effectively capture the essence of loneliness than Olivia Laing's *The Lonely City: Adventures in the Art of Being Alone*. In her book, Laing recounts her story of moving from the United Kingdom to New York, falling in love with a man and yet soon after finding herself "unexpectedly unhinged."[1] Laing's first years in New York are characterized by a lingering loneliness, "a feeling of separation, of being walled off or penned in," this "combine[d] with a sense of near-unbearable exposure."[2] Integrating autobiography, cultural criticism and social science, Laing's work is among the most poignant in a recent stream of books and articles dedicated to the theme of loneliness.

Much has been written about loneliness in past years, as researchers, journalists and writers such as Laing attempt to grapple with an aspect of the human condition about which we are acutely aware in modern life. Loneliness is a state with which many struggle, but there is surprisingly little constructive dialogue on this topic. Why is this? Laing offers several responses. First, individuals are fearful of exploring the topic, given that it is "hard to describe."[3] She references the psychiatrist Frieda Fromm-Reichmann, who writes, "The writer who wishes to elaborate on loneliness is faced with a serious terminological handicap: Loneliness seems to be such a painful, frightening experience that people do practically everything to avoid it."[4] A second consideration is that loneliness turns others away. It is possible to sense when others are lonely, as they shut off and attempt to protect themselves. This makes it increasingly difficult for lonely people to emerge from this state, creating what Laing considers a "virtuous cycle [...] a prophylactic that inhibits contact, no matter how badly contact is desired."[5]

Other considerations relate to what we have already seen in Part II. In a hyperconnected society, it is assumed that individuals are usually connected, this simply being the default state in our daily communications. Moreover, given the propensity for millennials to share what they do, terms such as openness and inclusivity come to dominate thinking about how we should live. Loneliness seems antithetical to the openness that we so value.

While few contemporary writers specifically investigate loneliness in modern work, much is written on a closely related topic: that of mental health. For young people, this is an enormous issue, and I fear that it is only getting worse. Thankfully, many initiatives seek to address mental health issues with this demographic and society more broadly. The Bell Let's Talk initiative, an annual Canadian campaign, is one of the best examples that I've seen of public advocacy on this topic. Each year, on Bell Let's Talk Day, the company donates five cents for every text, call or social media contribution on the topic, this raising approximately $6 million in the last year. The campaign has been tremendously effective among my peers, there always being considerable discussion on Facebook about mental health whenever the campaign takes place.

In the United Kingdom, the Royal Society for Public Health (RSPH) has been vocal about mental health issues, specifically through its recent #StatusofMind campaign. In a recent study, the RSPH finds that "rates of anxiety and depression have increased 70% in the past 25 years."[6] But as unfortunate as the increase in mental health problems among millennials is, this trend should be of little surprise to us. I cannot help but think that loneliness is a driving factor behind today's mental health issues. My sense is moreover that for many, loneliness stems not only from social isolation but rather from incongruity between perceptions of reality in one's own life and that of others.

As previously discussed, today's recent graduates and young professionals often see themselves in perpetual competition against their colleagues, where stillness is considered antithetical to the adaptability necessary for a rapidly changing world. Moreover, as we've seen through thinkers such as Turkle, performance and identity are frequently conflated. These and other themes are relevant to a critical examination of loneliness. In addressing this topic, I will first suggest that loneliness arises through excessive awareness of the lives that others lead, whether or not awareness is based on reality.

Building on this first point is a second consideration: that millennials begin to *expect* that their lives can progress in a manner that they have carefully predetermined based on the information at their fingertips. And finally, given the competitiveness of the modern world—reflected in the belief that modern education is ultimately a means to securing good jobs—people feel that their successes and failures in their lives and career pursuits are purely *theirs*. This leaves us feeling anchorless, not just alone but also *deficient* based on comparisons to others, to what we expect to be doing and to what we could be doing if only we wanted to. These chasms are conducive to loneliness, for they suggest that we cannot measure up—that we are perpetually in a state of deficiency. The problem is that this obstructs aloneness, which serves as a basis for solitude.

## COMPARISON AND LONELINESS

The first consideration—that of exposure to lives we perceive others to be leading—is addressed by Stephen Marche in *The Atlantic*, where he writes that through Facebook "we have the lovely smoothness of a seemingly social machine. Everything's so simple: status updates, pictures, your wall [...] But the price of this smooth sociability is a constant compulsion to assert one's own happiness, one's own fulfillment."[7] This certainly resonates. As a member of the Global Shapers Community, I have on many occasions felt rather lonely when looking at what my friends and colleagues in the network present themselves as doing.

Recently, while sitting in my flat, the rain pouring against the sunroof on a typically overcast and gloomy day, I scrolled through pictures shared on Facebook from a "SHAPE North America" conference, a gathering of several hundred Global Shapers from Mexico, the United States and Canada taking place over several days in Toronto and Ottawa. In one particularly representative image of the event, several individuals convened one night in a ballroom, one person playing the piano as others sat together, listening, contemplating and sharing in laughter. Other images consisted of individuals participating in workshops with Canadian ministers and other political leaders, taking early-morning bus rides between the two cities and generally seeming to have an excellent time together. On my side of the Atlantic, the weekend consisted largely of working through a lengthy but important book that had for long been on my desk and that needed to be tackled.

It is difficult indeed to resist venturing onto Facebook (or other platforms), even though each foray into others' lives interrupts and dampens more than it enriches present activity. After nearly every log-off, I cannot help but feel a subtle diminishment in the quality of my day. As I briefly imagine what others are doing—whether in Toronto, Ottawa, Jerusalem or London—negative questions come to mind: "Why am I *only* reading a book?"; "Why am I not at this conference?"; "Am I really learning as much here at home as I could somewhere else?" Sometimes these questions are unconscious, more so a *sense* that something is missing. I am then caught between two worlds, no longer focused on the present activity, attention allocated to these other streams of thought.

Much of the loneliness that I see nowadays is based on unrealistic expectations, in which people believe—given what others *say* they are doing—that their own lives will progress in a similarly linear and smooth manner. The comparisons are based on incomplete information: we see what is going well, but have very little clue as to what lives *really* look like. We might see a person succeeding, building companies, earning interesting degrees and traveling the world, and yet not know that beneath all of this lies considerable strife or uncertainty. Floating in the wake of the appearance of success might be troubled relationships, financial stress and self-doubt. These parts of life are rarely if ever presented online. They are only to be discovered through in-person conversation, and even then only when individuals are honest with themselves and others.

We provide very little room in our society for human messiness—the reality that there are problems behind every person's door. This is reflected in countless discussions with colleagues, where they admit intense frustration when their lives do not feel "on track" at the same time as their colleagues appear to be pressing forward. A key reason for this, I think, is that our understanding of what progression entails is deficient. The concept is for many a perpetual moving-forward in the fulfillment of goals and ambitions. We are called to achieve, particularly in the realm of the career. What we need is a more realistic account of human foresight, in which we recognize that unpredictable life circumstances might impede the outcomes that we envision for ourselves. This would help us imagine more realistic and authentic life trajectories. Frustration and thwarted efforts are often exactly what we need, these being helpful in the articulation of what kind of life is worth living.

Bandura writes that "some of the most important determinants of life paths often arise through the most trivial of circumstances,"[8] and provides a wide range of examples in which chance transforms individuals' lives. One of these is particularly noteworthy:

> In his Nobel lecture, Herbert Brown (1980) recounts how he happened to decide to pursue doctoral research in the rare field of boron hydrides. As a baccalaureate gift, his girlfriend presented him with a copy of the book, The Hydrides of Boron and Silicon, which launched his interest in the subject. This was during the Depression when money was scarce. She happened to select this particular chemistry book undesignedly because it was the least expensive one ($2.06) available in the university bookstore. Had his girlfriend been a bit more affluent, Brown's research career would in all likelihood have taken a different route.[9]

Bandura suggests that a person's values, skills and emotional ties, among other factors, help them take advantage of chance encounters or resist ones that might send a life in directions that could lead to personal ruin. Thus, it is not that chance is always beneficial, nor that it spreads evenly across the population. It is more likely that chance favors those already in positions of privilege. Those born into wealthy families are more likely to be exposed to ideas, people and places in which chance will benefit the individual (say, through opportunities for jobs).

Conversely, those born into more difficult circumstances must combat against influences, many unforeseen, which could send their lives in the wrong direction. The overarching point in all of this is that chance is an important part of life. Human beings' control over the direction of life is limited. But it is possible that circumstances that initially bring frustration—Herbert Brown, for instance, coming of age during the Depression—can actually be of immense benefit in the long term.

A challenge for us is therefore not to look at frustration in the pursuit of goals and aspirations as spelling the end. We mustn't bow to the pressure to continually perform. Indeed, the contrast between present circumstances and envisioned futures can produce feelings of intense anxiety and loneliness, particularly when individuals see themselves as not measuring up to their peer benchmark. What individuals say they are doing is rarely reflective of reality.

Loneliness takes place as individuals compare themselves uncritically with others, as well as with expectations as to how their own lives should unfold. And it arises in another manner: that of awareness of the lives that individuals could lead, *if only they wanted*. In my conversations with millennials over past years, they consistently remark on the importance of keeping options open, in order to maintain as much flexibility as possible in career development. This is sometimes referred to as "cross-sectoral thinking," in which individuals consider transitioning across public, private and nonprofit sectors.

I believe there are a number of reasons for this focus on career mobility. First, there is widespread recognition that in order to solve "wicked problems," individuals must gather knowledge from across disciplines. For instance, in order to tackle climate change, environmentalists cannot work in isolation. Instead, they must speak with economists and financiers, philosophers and sociologists, among other professionals. Second, cross-sectoral thinking serves as a defense mechanism of sorts, in that it insulates individuals from harm in case particular industries collapse. It is, in other words, a matter of adaptability to potential unforeseen circumstances. And third, our societal interest in mobility is perhaps a result of the average life span increasing across Western society, this providing workers with opportunities to explore more widely before they decide on what they are truly intent on doing in their lives.

Though sampling from a variety of industries can broaden one's perspective—this is, after all, one of the main perks of the consulting industry— a potential negative consequence is that an individual will spend too much time considering options and not actually commit to anything. In the modern age, the grass always seems to be greener on the other side, and options are always available to us. In his book *What Money Can't Buy: The Moral Limits of Markets*, the philosopher Michael Sandel writes about this phenomenon, remarking that we live in a marketplace society in which individuals begin to think about even the most human dimensions of their lives in terms of markets.[10]

It is of course true that millennials (as is the case with any other generational cohort) do not have the ability to pursue whatever careers they desire. A plethora of factors, social, cultural and economic, shape individuals' life paths whether they are aware of this or not. Individuals born into wealthy families on the East Coast of the United States, in which both parents attended Ivy League universities, obviously have much greater life prospects than those born into deprived rural communities in the Midwest. Choice is fundamentally social. Even the most ardent of individualists are influenced by things that they cannot fully control.

We are less mobile than we imagine. As an example, we can look at progression from low- to high-skill forms of work within given occupations. The idea of *occupational stasis*, documented by researchers from the University of Sydney, captures what I mean.[11] In a series of studies, University of Sydney researchers discovered that it is rare for individuals to move to high-skill forms of work when their starting point is a low-skill job. This is not surprising, but it is deeply troubling, showing that early life experiences and the choices we make—often without awareness of their significance—narrow future life trajectories.

Despite this, individuals whom I have interviewed and observed over past years are seldom satisfied with the work that they undertake in the moment. Even when feeling fulfilled in their present circumstances, they suggest that it might be better to work elsewhere. New environments would seem to provide better opportunities to develop skills and self-actualize. No matter how satisfying the present might be, the question is usually "What next?"

Universities contribute to this short-termism, notably through one-year master's degrees, which, much like MBA programs, do not seem to offer a lot in the form of rigorous intellectual content. This is not to say that short-termism does not have its benefits. Spending time with a variety of people in different places, industries and programs can broaden a person's horizons. Rather, a central issue in this mindset is that individuals *delay* making important decisions. In the name of adaptability, they balance multiple activities rather than say definitively, "This is what I care about, and thus what I will devote the majority of my time to." The hors d'oeuvres platter offers many delicious treats, and so it is difficult to progress to the main course.

Persistent consideration of potential career paths diminishes our sense of purpose in our present work. Spreading ourselves across multiple activities in the name of adaptability, and perpetually aware of what other opportunities might arise, it becomes difficult to establish roots in a single place. For the millennials who *do* commit the vast majority of their time to a single employer, for instance, they look to their comparatively peripatetic peers and wonder whether this sort of life is more strategic. This psychological disposition, in which adaptability reigns supreme, means that it becomes difficult to enjoy the benefits of good work dedicated to a particular craft.

Instead, we tend to cut our work into many pieces, each piece tied to a project. These projects change relatively frequently. As such it becomes difficult to build a solid foundation upon which we can stand. Conventional wisdom would nowadays suggest that these multiple projects are advantageous for the individual, allowing for rapid transitions from one activity to the next as we express ourselves in our multiple dimensions. And yet, it is *this* mindset that contributes to loneliness, the projects and connections usually plentiful but shallow. The sociologist Richard Sennett, writing in his book *The Craftsman*, provides insightful remarks on what it means to undertake good work, saying that "we should be suspicious of claims for innate, untrained talent [...] Going over an action again and again, by contrast, enables self-criticism."[12]

The three forms of comparison that I have now described leave individuals feeling anchorless, pulled away from their inner selves. Our perpetual comparison——part of the fabric of modern lives, brings about loneliness. Compounding loneliness is the decline of community life. The decline of communities is catalogued in Robert Putnam's book *Bowling Alone*, which outlines the weakening of associational activities and of social capital within the United States. (A more recent Putnam book, *Our Kids*, provides further evidence of the decline of social capital in the United States.) It should become apparent that individuals are increasingly left to fend for themselves. In their book *The Wellness Syndrome*, André Spicer and Carl Cederström use the term "free-agents."[13] It is the responsibility of the individual to find jobs. When they are unsuccessful, they have only themselves to blame. Entrepreneurship, its own buzzword in modern society, is similarly troublesome: it has "become the very reflection of rampant individualism that our society champions wholeheartedly," write Navneet Khinda and Dongwoo Kim in the *Globe and Mail*.[14]

Given this defective individualism, it becomes difficult for individuals to discuss their loneliness (and mental health challenges) with others. A significant portion of my peers, though conventionally successful and seemingly composed in their daily endeavors, experience considerable anxiety in private. I'm no longer surprised when friends share with me their battles with depression. Beyond talking with their families, it is difficult for people to display actual vulnerability, for such openness is often construed as weakness precisely in a world where individuals must "hustle" in order to keep pace with the crowd.

These sorts of honest conversations are the hallmark of friendship, but they are difficult to come by when a marketplace framework pervades thinking about the most significant facets of human life. As such, individuals are left with two options: live truthfully and risk falling behind in the eyes of their colleagues, or live inauthentically and receive praise for their performances (while suffering internally).

## INTEGRITY IN ALONENESS

Perceived inadequacy in comparison to others, and to what we expect to be doing, serves as a barrier to aloneness. Psychologically, these sorts of questions are ever present, making it difficult for individuals to spend time with themselves. When individuals have time and space to be alone, they try to fill this with opportunities to connect—that is, to *do* things that contribute to a sense of progression in their lives.

To be alone is, in other words, accompanied by nervousness and restlessness. It is of course always possible in the modern world to fill empty space with things to do: with Facebook, videos and texts. Loneliness has become the default state for us in our inner worlds.

Aloneness is thus impeded in several important ways. The first reason pertains to *fear* of loneliness. We struggle, in other words, to escape from a framework in which connectedness is the default manner of existence. The second reason is that when we are alone, we think about what we could spend time *doing*. And the third reason is that the feelings of anxiety and uncertainty produced in loneliness make it difficult to change course, individuals not knowing where to find help in order to cultivate their relationships with aloneness.

For many, the thought of spending time alone evokes fear. When friends and colleagues appear to be racing forward, acquiring new experiences, spending time alone is viewed as a disadvantage. Put differently, aloneness represents stagnation, if not retreat or decline. Many friends, in our conversations about solitude and aloneness, wonder whether such activities are not rather reclusive. In place of this, it has been proposed to me on numerous occasions that a focus on *community* might be more fitting for my purposes. I can see what these friends are saying: there are cases in which aloneness really *is* a matter of withdrawal from the world. Moreover, as traditional community ties weaken—as Putnam indicates in his research—it is important that we find ways to bring individuals from all walks of life together, so that they can meet and talk in the public realm about their hopes, fears and aspirations. I am not unaware of these important considerations. That said, what concerns me is that spending time alone has become a practice to be *avoided* given the rise in popularity of concepts such as community and belonging. Several examples illustrate this point.

The first of these is personal. Ironically, the writing of this very book was delayed by my own inability to sit still and write in aloneness in early mornings and on weekends, this driven by a need to keep up with client demands and an addiction of sorts that I had developed to traveling—to constantly being on the move for work. Prior to moving back to England from Canada, I traveled frequently between the two countries, usually for meetings. For much of the last year, I would fly back and forth about once per month, if not more frequently. Once having returned to Canada, it would not be long—several days, if not hours—before I booked a new trip. While in England, I traveled as frequently as possible. Most of these travels pertained to meetings, it being my aim to maintain the relationships formed in both countries.

Focused on constant activity, hitting deadlines, setting goals and thinking about the future, it became difficult to spend time with myself on weekends and evenings. Restlessness became a state of mind. Even when it was possible to be on my own, I booked coffees and other engagements that prevented this from happening. I was unable to disengage from a "doing" mentality.

A friend recently wrote to me over Facebook about his attempt to set time aside for aloneness: "I've been doing a 30 min walk every night without headphones/podcasts—very helpful." Beyond this, however, I must work hard to find examples of friends who spend time in aloneness, and who do *not* then feel compelled to share these kinds of activities with others through platforms such as Facebook. To take a solo hike or a neighborhood walk, to go to the movies or to a restaurant on one's own or to simply sit at one's kitchen table and read—these are by and large activities that we try to avoid.

When spending time alone, it is difficult indeed to shut off, aloneness interrupted by a myriad of texts, e-mails and things to do. Alone time is beset by an inability to sit still, uninterrupted, in which we spend time thinking or writing about any particular thing for several minutes. As one colleague shared with me several months ago, the phrase "Let me sit on this, and I'll get back to you," is all but dead. To utter these words in modern society would be strange indeed (the expectation now being that we must respond quickly to whatever people ask of us)! Spending time *with ourselves*, in contemplation, is viewed as antisocial. We see this perhaps no more clearly than in the significant number of individuals who, when on their own in public settings, instinctively pull out a phone.

A friend once recommended that I play a game while on the train: look around and determine what proportion of individuals is not on their phones, not listening to music, not eating or not drinking (several decades ago, a fifth option would have been to look for those not smoking a cigarette). It is unlikely that individuals playing this game will find more than 25 percent of people in a train car not doing one of these four things. In other words, rarely can we now find people looking out the window, perhaps bored, perhaps daydreaming, perhaps reflecting on some aspect of life—basically, not doing anything.

It takes time before a person can unwind and transition from thinking about what they want or need to do, to thinking about what kinds of things are truly worth (or not worth) valuing, reflecting on, or doing. When spending time alone, the lowest-hanging fruit for self-reflection is that of thinking about goals and achievements, these being highly practical things. We think administratively, about our lists, as this maintains the semblance of achievement. Yet this practicality impedes reflection on *principles*, as Tawney tells us.

A colleague recently asked, toward the end of a coffee meeting, what it is that I have *noticed* of late in my work (and life more generally). Responses to this simple question are indeed reflective of the extent to which individuals pay attention in their lives: to the quality of observations that they make about the things happening around them. The challenge with constant action is that it reduces capacity to notice. And the inability to notice, I think, is the cause of much personal trouble, such as poor career decisions, relationships gone sour (which were never really suitable in the first place!), and a general lack of curiosity regarding one's daily existence.

It is in aloneness that we can consider the questions most on our minds and listen for the questions waiting to emerge. Aloneness provides space in which it is possible to *hear* responses, some more precise than others and some that remain embryonic, in need of clearer formulation. We are able to reflect in aloneness on our meaningful interactions with friends and colleagues.

Earlier, we encountered the theologian Whitehead in his commentary on the relationship between knowledge and wisdom. It is only through romance, precision and generalization that a person can develop active knowledge. Knowledge gradually becomes wisdom when the former is handled with particular care and style. It is not merely *what* one knows that matters but *how* one handles what one knows. In the modern world, a myriad of interruptions hinder the cultivation of the sort of style to which Whitehead refers. And it is *style* that I believe is, paradoxically, largely unattainable in the world that we inhabit. Style requires that individuals consider what they learn from others and make sense of knowledge *in their own terms*, in a fashion that is true to who they are as individuals.

This formation takes time. More specifically, style requires careful study, practice and reflection. But in the modern world, self-presentation takes the place of style. Loneliness is thus not only a contributor to anxiety among millennials. It is, in addition, a barrier to spending extended periods of time alone with ourselves, in which we can make sense of our lives, in our own words. It should be to our collective dismay that, as we condone and indulge in an endless series of interruptions and comparisons, it becomes more difficult to live in accordance with who we are as unique individuals.

## NOTES

1  Olivia Laing, *The Lonely City: Adventures in the Art of Being Alone* (Edinburgh: Canongate, 2016), 12.
2  Ibid., 17.
3  Ibid., 24.
4  Ibid.
5  Ibid., 28.
6  Royal Society for Public Health, "#StatusOfMind," 2017. Available from: https://www.rsph.org.uk/our-work/policy/social-media-and-young-people-s-mental-health-and-wellbeing.html.
7  Stephen Marche, "Is Facebook Making Us Lonely?" *Atlantic*, May 2012. Available from: https://www.theatlantic.com/magazine/archive/2012/05/is-facebook-making-us-lonely/308930/.
8  Albert Bandura, "The Psychology of Chance Encounters and Life Paths," *American Psychologist* 37, no. 7 (1982): 749. Available from: http://www.itari.in/categories/higherpurpose/psychology_of_life.pdf.
9  Ibid.
10  Michael Sandel, *What Money Can't Buy: The Moral Limits of Markets* (New York: Farrar, Straus and Giroux, 2012).
11  Serena Yu et al., *Working Paper: Understanding the Nature of Vocations Today: Exploring Labour Market Pathways*, Workplace Research Centre University of Sydney, October 22, 2012.

12  Richard Sennett, *The Craftsman* (London: Penguin Books, 2008), 37–38.

13  Carl Cederström and André Spicer, *The Wellness Syndrome* (Cambridge: Polity, 2015).

14  Dongwoo Kim and Navneet Khinda, "Selfishness Defines Gen Y Entrepreneurs," *Globe and Mail*, March 28, 2014. Available from: https://beta.theglobeandmail.com/news/national/education/gen-y-entrepreneurs-its-not-about-you/article17693850/?ref=http://www.theglobeandmail.com&.

# CHAPTER 8

# SOLITUDE AND ALONENESS

The trouble with writing about solitude is that our discussion about this concept usually takes place within a framework that *itself* needs to be questioned. The framework that I refer to is that of the self-interested individual focused on maximizing productivity. Looking from this vantage point, the individual strives for efficiencies in the name of economic gain. Using this framework, solitude is seen as one of two things. On the one hand, as a means to refresh oneself so that one can more effectively perform in work. On the other, as a way to get away from the hustle and bustle of modern life, that is, as a *refuge* from modern life.

Neither of these conceptions of solitude is satisfactory. In this chapter, I will begin with a description of solitude, discussing what I believe it is and, equally, what I believe it is not. Following this, I will examine several considerations that can enhance solitude. I put forward the idea that despite various pressures, it is critical that individuals *resist* the urge to share so openly and immediately with each other, reflecting instead on the value of cultivating a private self.

## DISTINGUISHING SOLITUDE FROM ALONENESS

Aloneness does not imply solitude. It is possible to be alone and connected. While walking through our public parks, fellow strollers are often alone and yet tapping away on their cellphones. The "tethered self" makes this state of existence an unfortunate reality. Seldom, it seems, are individuals fully present in their aloneness. We are instead perpetually scattered, pulled in a myriad of directions.

Several examples can help differentiate solitude from aloneness. Recently, I met for coffee with a friend on a sunny Friday evening. While approaching the coffee shop, I noticed she was not on any device (a unique and encouraging sight, of course). As I apologized for running slightly behind, she remarked that no apology was needed—it was enjoyable for her to people-watch. In the minutes prior to my arrival, this friend was able to spend time observing others without reverting to her phone or to things that needed doing. This friend was alone, but this example is not yet reflective of what I mean by solitude. That is because in this example, aloneness is fleeting: it is soon to be interrupted with social engagement. Put differently, in distinguishing solitude from aloneness, it is important to consider the *duration* of a given activity, as well as *closeness* to other human beings.

What if we are to take the example of a local sitting in a park underneath a tree, some distance away from the main walking trails, reading a book or scribbling in their journal? This person's aloneness is purposeful. But while the person in this example *is* alone, removed from a crowd and engaged in what appears to be reflective activity (writing in a journal), physical description does not fully communicate what solitude entails. Physical descriptions, in other words, are necessary but insufficient for describing solitude in the manner that I believe is sufficiently robust. Solitude must take into account psychological and philosophical features, which I will briefly describe.

Psychological descriptions are prominent in contemporary accounts of solitude. The article "The Virtues of Isolation," published in *The Atlantic*, is a case in point. The author writes that "under the right circumstances, choosing to spend time alone can be a huge psychological boon."[1] Moreover, "The difference between solitude as rejuvenation and solitude as suffering is the quality of self-reflection that one can generate while in it, and the ability to come back to social groups when one wants to."[2] Many contemporary accounts of solitude focus on its psychosocial benefits. It is only through solitude, for example, that individuals can tap into their inner selves and become more creative, more alert and more productive. This means that solitude ultimately helps individuals get ahead in their work, fulfill themselves and interact more effectively in groups.

While interesting, I find there is something missing in these psychosocial accounts of solitude. Too often a focus on psychology in accounts of solitude is really just a matter of "how best to improve productivity through *neuroscience*." We think that solitude is important because it contributes to a person's well-being or because it allows for associational connections between the left and right parts of the brain. Certainly, how a person thinks in solitude is of utmost importance. That said, appeals to neuroscience do not capture the role of *intention* in solitude. We might understand the neurological processes underlying solitude—and even then, an educated layperson will have a hard time telling the good from the bad in the scientific research presented—but neuroscience does not get us closer to the intention behind the personal search.

Neither do these psychological appeals fully address notions of truth, honesty, patience and frustration in the search. The frame that I wish to provide for solitude is therefore *philosophical*. I will now outline what I mean by a philosophical approach to solitude.

In talking about solitude, we needn't concern ourselves too much with ends. What matters in solitude is not that the solitary walker returns from a walk having found a solution to a problem, however pressing this problem might have been. Solitude as a means to performance is not what we should be focusing on. Rather, we should direct our attention to a process of a certain *kind*. Specifically, I view solitude as a philosophical practice, in which we have the needed time and space for considering how questions of significance to us are to be formulated. We are from this able to reflect on potential responses and *hear* what we have to say.

It is a process in which responses might not be found. But the possible, if not likely, dead ends encountered in the search should be of little significance to individuals who spend time in solitude. It is that we *intend* to search that matters: that we are aware of the need to more carefully formulate questions, in which subtle alterations can affect how we think about ourselves, what matters to us and how we should live. This, I think, is a key distinction between aloneness and solitude. It is possible for a person to be physically alone and engaged in some kind of reflection, perhaps reflection on their week and on which of their goals they have yet to accomplish. And yet that individual might not be in solitude as I understand it. Solitude must take place in physical aloneness, but it is more importantly a search in one's aloneness. More specifically, it is a search and clarification of questions pertaining to what it means to live a good life, accompanied by patience and honesty in hearing what emerges.

Solitude involves purpose, but it is not a purpose to *do*. The purpose is rather to contemplate. In the modern age, one gravitates toward solitude, I think, having found that their hyperconnectedness prevents them from engaging in uninterrupted contemplation. We are encouraged to think but mostly in a shallow manner. It becomes apparent that fast answers are readily available and yet deeply unsatisfactory. Many individuals will, of course, never arrive at this point of contemplative departure. Many people—millennials especially, but also others—are content with life as is, viewing the sort of contemplation to which I refer as requiring too much effort, for such contemplation does not always help us achieve outcomes. The rewards are unclear in the short term. In fact, it is possible that this formulation and reformulation of questions will *set one back* in one's intended progress. The chance of falling behind is unsettling. But there are few questions more difficult than "What do *I* think?" or "What *really* matters to me?"

It is not always apparent why we should spend time in solitude. The lack of encouragement in the modern world for solitude obstructs many who may sense its significance. After all, solitude requires that time be spent away from the hustle of modern life so that we can listen carefully to ourselves. This suggests that solitude requires that a person be a contrarian. This is hard work. It is difficult to transition away from thoughts about practical things: to-do lists, goals, ambitions and so on. This is partly why millennials, based on my observations over past years, are fearful of solitude—responses do *not* come quickly! The seriousness and slowness involved in solitude run counter to how we feel we must live in order to progress. And so this scares us.

But it is only through extended time spent alone that individuals can listen carefully to themselves. The individuals whom I have encountered over past years who spend time in solitude seem to understand this, and they are clear with others that their time alone is sacred. This directness with others requires courage, for to consider time alone as sacred is often construed as *not wanting to socialize*, or as lacking social connections. One must demonstrate restraint when a myriad of pressures risk solitude being interpreted as social isolation—that is, as loneliness.

Because of practical realities (like jobs, schooling or parenting), the majority of individuals cannot simply go and spend extended periods of time alone. Under intense pressure to progress in the various facets of their lives and careers, people will naturally look at solitude and wonder how it is conducive to their growth. Solitude will at first seem unattainable. Socioeconomic considerations also influence a person's ability to engage in meaningful solitude. That said, most individuals, I think, have the capacity to *decide* that solitude is important to them.

Solitude is indeed a commitment, one not to be taken lightly. It means, perhaps, that we turn down opportunities to spend time with friends, to go to parties or to networking events. This requires personal restraint as well as a vision of what solitude offers us. It helps if we value the often intangible benefits that solitude brings, above and beyond the immediacy that is part of modern culture. I will now briefly consider the benefits of solitude in order to make a stronger case for its practice.

## CONSIDERATIONS IN SOLITUDE

Solitude allows for honesty in our self-reflection, but this means that we must bring seriousness to its practice. Time spent in solitude is not to be approached lightheartedly, particularly when time constraints make such time precious.

What matters is not that we are serious in finding answers to our questions, for it is possible that the questions themselves might not be framed correctly. Rather, we must be serious in the *consideration* given to the questions that we ask ourselves—how they are to be framed most effectively. This is far from a straightforward process in which questions move quickly to solutions. Questions can be at first vague and difficult to formulate. And the questions that we really need to ask are not always apparent from the beginning of the search.

In order to be honest in our self-reflection, we must ask the question "Why?" and further to this, listen carefully to the responses that emerge. A person might, for instance, believe that they would like to enter politics. As they consider why this is the case, the first response might be that politicians can influence public policy. It could also be that a politician gets to interact with many different people across a constituency, and that this interaction is seen as enjoyable. Or, it could simply be that politics provides financial stability (at least until your party falls!). However, as this person pays closer attention to why politics beckons, it is possible that *fame* surfaces as a driving force.

This person might realize that their convictions are not nearly as clear as previously imagined. It could be that when reflecting on conversations with friends and colleagues, they realize that their responses to questions about what issues matter in politics are in fact quite weak. This could all be very telling. It is also, of course, possible that reflection on the reasons for entering politics *strengthens* this person's conviction that this really is something worth pursuing. Regardless of the outcome, solitude provides the time and space for this kind of nuanced reflection. Solitude involves, in the other words, the repeated asking of the question "Why?"—and careful listening to the responses. The questioning continues until one can go no further. Solitude, and only solitude, allows for this kind of interrogation of self.

One might at this point ask how individuals *become* honest with themselves in the manner described above. There is no silver bullet. Honesty requires courage, patience and perceptiveness, but these qualities are not easily developed. Certainly, it helps to have role models—the wise teachers, as Whitehead describes in his book—who provide us with a sense of what it looks like for these qualities to be exercised in person. But the sincerest of answers to this question would be that these qualities must be practiced: they can only be developed over time. Indeed, when approaching solitude with intention, we can overcome the constraints that make this practice difficult. Solitude is largely a matter of repetition.

A second consideration related to the practice of solitude is that individuals must embrace frustration and demonstrate patience. These points go hand in hand. There should be little expectation that solitude will provide the answers that we seek. To the contrary, solitude can be a *source* of frustration, for it can be difficult to even arrive at a place where one begins to consider and formulate questions effectively. Given the hyperconnectedness to which millennials are accustomed, it should not be expected that individuals will transition rapidly and smoothly into time spent in solitude. Hours often pass before we can begin to think meaningfully about our lives. Indeed, when we expect fast answers, the benefits of solitude will only be delayed. We must therefore be serious but patient in solitude, questioning and listening as responses emerge in their own time.

Of course, patience is hard to muster given the immediacy of modern communication. As Turkle writes, the greater the volume of communication that individuals send into their networks, the greater the weight of communication received in turn. Volume of responses is a key measure by which individuals gauge their productivity and, unfortunately, their value in the modern world. Solitude cannot be measured in this way. Indeed, it is impossible to quantify or expedite it. The rewards of solitude are immaterial; it is only possible for individuals to make sense of them over time.

Certainly it is possible that individuals, used to ongoing comparison with others, will turn away from solitude as they begin to encounter frustration. They will wonder why it is that *their* lives involve uncertainty and messiness while others' lives appear to progress so smoothly. Further to this, they might wonder how it is that others don't spend time in solitude—confronting themselves about their lives—and yet still achieve success. It is possible, when looking at how others present themselves, for one to believe that lives unfold in this kind of linear fashion. But no human life is without its trials. We might be inclined to think otherwise—forgetting that performances do not reflect reality—but this generation is no less human than others. It is because of the reality of human limitedness that patience and frustration must be embraced as vital components of solitude.

A third consideration with solitude is that its results are *not* to be shared. Indeed, to present the fruits of solitude to others would be to misunderstand the essence of the activity. Far too often, millennials write on social media about what they have "learned" during conferences, travels and other activities in which they might have spent some time alone. These reflections are frequently half-baked, more promotional than they are substantive. Still, I observe many friends and acquaintances who, after having spent some time alone, wish to immediately share what they have learned. Or, they might *want* to have something to share, in order to maintain the self-illusion of importance as well as ensure that the activity can be measured (in this case through likes and comments on their reflections). Neither of these above options is advantageous. In fact, there is little that could be more deleterious to solitude, for the fruits of solitude do not ripen in the short term. The value of solitude is not to be found in what it *delivers*. What we learn in solitude is not to be shared in the short term.

Solitude therefore requires a sense as to what should be kept private. Millennials really struggle with this idea, the modern world favoring concepts such as openness and transparency. When interesting ideas spring to mind, and as one takes part in new experiences, the path of least resistance is to share these with others. This sharing then allows for peer validation—likes and shares—which suggests that one was correct to share in the first place. But there is considerable value in holding on to thoughts, allowing them to develop in their own time. As was previously mentioned, we seldom say that we will "sit on this" when others request our perspective on a question. To utter these words in modern society is basically heretical. But such pause is paramount in our world, for it enriches thinking and provides us with depth.

A sense of the private undergirds solitude, expanding rather than limiting freedom to engage in critical self-examination. In asking "Why?" it is not necessarily the case that all responses, when we listen carefully, will be positive. It is very difficult for individuals to confront themselves. We might realize that the lives that we envision are not reflective of our identity, that in listening closely to our inner dialogue, something feels off. Similarly, we might admit that we are unhappy with our partner, our work, our education, or that there are aspects of our conduct that must improve. The formulation and consideration of questions—and the process of listening to responses—does not unfold predictably and linearly. It is only in privacy that this process can evolve freely. To expect or wish to share outcomes would hinder the maturation of our thinking.

Finally, it is possible that individuals, in their solitude, will occasionally experience loneliness. Solitude and loneliness are often presented as being mutually exclusive; however, this distinction is not always as clear as it seems. Hara Estroff Marano, writing in *Psychology Today* notes, "Loneliness is a negative state, marked by a sense of isolation. One feels that something is missing. It is possible to be with people and still feel lonely—perhaps the most bitter form of loneliness."[3] In stark opposition to this, "Solitude is the state of being alone without being lonely. It is a positive and constructive state of engagement with oneself. Solitude is desirable, a state of being alone where you provide yourself wonderful and sufficient company."[4] This account reflects most contemporary definitions of solitude and loneliness. One is positive, the other negative. One involves wholeness, the other a sense that something is missing. Solitude is not as straightforward a concept as this. It is not always positive for the individual, even when the individual chooses to spend time in solitude.

As we have already discussed, solitude requires courage. An individual must first overcome pressure to remain connected in the modern world. When in solitude, one must demonstrate patience, embrace frustration and maintain a sense of the private. Overarching these qualities is the reality that solitude allows for the confrontation of self, as one formulates questions and listens carefully to the responses. Solitude is a serious, not trivial, activity. It is indeed a practice upon which one can improve over time. As such, it should be of little surprise to readers that solitude sometimes involves loneliness.

Few people, as I have found over past years, strive to spend time in solitude, whether in the countryside, in their homes or in between. For those who do, it can be difficult to discuss this with others, the expectation being that friends and colleagues might find the interest in solitude to be rather strange or antisocial. Indeed, we may experience loneliness when confronting ourselves, the question "Why?" among the hardest questions that we can ask.

These considerations help show why solitude and loneliness are not mutually exclusive. This does not weaken the case for solitude. Loneliness is in this sense productive and to be embraced, for it sometimes indicates that individuals are on the right path in their solitude. The initial frustration that solitude provokes can, in the long term, provide immense benefits, ones that are incalculable in the present. The search for questions and responses that occurs while in solitude is demanding, and so it is only natural that this occasionally produces uncertainty and loneliness in one's life. This is, however, the kind of self worth cultivating.

## SOLITUDE IN PRACTICE

Solitude, as a *search* in aloneness, involves consideration as to which questions are worth asking, in addition to the reasons why. Outcomes, if we are to use this term, will shift as question-formulation evolves. So how are millennials to engage in solitude, particularly given the hyperconnected modern world? I suggest at multiple points in this chapter that many individuals will either not perceive the significance of solitude, or simply not wish to engage in this even when aware of potential benefits. To spend time in solitude is, after all, brave given the culture of which we are a part. In addition to this, it is possible that pressures related to career progression will make solitude seem unachievable.

Given my past years of work with friends and colleagues in this demographic, many express interest in the idea of solitude. Although it can be difficult to explain why solitude is important—modern justification leaning toward ends such as efficiency—there is nevertheless an underlying sense among many that solitude *matters*.

With sufficient public discourse on this topic, I believe that it is possible to encourage more individuals to spend time with themselves, engaged in a purposeful search focused on formulating and responding to significant questions. An account of solitude now provided, I shall now discuss what I see as several key philosophical and political questions that pertain to solitude, as they relate to community, access and education.

## NOTES

1   Brent Crane, "The Virtues of Isolation," *The Atlantic*, March 30, 2017. Available from: https://www.theatlantic.com/health/archive/2017/03/the-virtues-of-isolation/521100/.

2   Ibid.

3   Hara Estroff Marano, "What Is Solitude?" *Psychology Today*, July 1, 2003. Available from: https://www.psychologytoday.com/articles/200307/what-is-solitude.

4   Ibid.

# CHAPTER 9

# ACCESS, COMMUNITY AND EDUCATION

Several important concerns must be addressed that pertain to access, community and education. These concerns have tugged at me throughout the writing of this book, so it would be irresponsible to neglect these in our present discussion on solitude.

The first concern pertains to access, in particular around the question "Who can access solitude?" and then "In what ways?" This is not only a socioeconomic question but also a political one. The second concern pertains to community. In conversations with colleagues over the course of my writing, several individuals have suggested that a focus on solitude comes at the expense of community. These colleagues believe it would be better to talk about how we can bring people together rather than encourage them to spend time in solitude. This line of thinking is, I believe, mistaken, but it nevertheless requires attention.

A third concern pertains to education, in that some will argue that it becomes very difficult for a person brought up in a modern education system, focused on jobs and skills, to learn how to spend time alone. This concern has merit, and so I will propose several ideas that universities in particular might wish to consider in order to provide their members with greater opportunities for solitude. I will address these three concerns in the order outlined above.

## SOLITUDE AND ACCESS

Earlier, in Part I, I briefly discussed the work of behavioral economists Sendhil Mullainathan and Eldar Shafir in their book *Scarcity*. The authors argue that material scarcity contributes to psychological scarcity, which they call the "scarcity trap." A "bandwidth tax" makes it difficult for individuals to dedicate their time and energy to nonimmediate needs, say, to longer-term goals and aspirations. A young single mother working in multiple jobs, for instance, must first ensure financial security before other tasks can be focused on (and even then, the mother might not have very much energy to waste thinking about other things, like what kind of job or career she might wish to be in). The scarcity trap concept is powerful, and I believe that it has implications for our discussion on solitude.

My first concern is that those with material advantages will have greater access to, and capability in, their solitude. Conversely, individuals in more difficult circumstances—say, without university educations or in low-paying jobs—may find it much more difficult to purposefully spend time in solitude. A second, and related, concern pertaining to access is that solitude could place responsibility on individuals for whatever struggles they encounter in their lives, in the way that we now see with the use of the term "entrepreneurship." In this sense, solitude becomes a convenient political device, individuals then feeling even lonelier than they might have been in the first place due to the added responsibility placed on them while they are struggling. I will first address the question of *how* one engages with the material at their disposal (knowledge, relationships and other life experiences) while in solitude and then consider the question of access *to* solitude. I will then briefly consider solitude as a political concept.

If solitude is a social concept, individuals developing autonomy as they make sense of what they think *as individuals* based on the experiences of which they are a part, then the supposed quality of these sorts of experiences might have some bearing on the practice of solitude. One might say that these experiences influence the kinds of questions that a person formulates in solitude. It could reasonably be argued that individuals with early life advantages would have richer material to work with in their solitude. Having taken part in a wide array of cultural and educational activities—say, trips around the world, participation in language courses or simply access to a large private collection of books—it would then be possible to formulate better questions in solitude.

This is perhaps a compelling argument to some, though ultimately I believe that it is misguided. A brief example helps show why. Not very long ago, I was part of a London book club involving about thirty millennials (though 15 to 20 would participate in any particular gathering). Many of the participants were Oxbridge graduates and, going even further back, many went to elite British private schools (though in Britain these are, strangely, called "public" schools; the North American equivalent of a public school is referred to in Britain as a "state" school). I was struck by how little *listening* took place in this book club, most participants wanting to get their turns in for sharing their own eloquently put opinions, and thus, frequently speaking past each other. Despite the good intentions of the organizer, I would leave wondering what was actually *said* during these conversations. Despite their privileged upbringings and fancy educations, their dialogue amounted to very little of real depth.

Though it is risky to make generalizations about those with significant early advantages in their lives, my personal experience suggests that these advantages are certainly not conducive to individuals understanding themselves or others. Extensive travels, the reading of books, language courses and other benefits provide intellectual enrichment, but they do not ensure the kind of realism-with-self that I have in mind. In some cases they actually *hinder* it, serving as means for cheap security. Material wealth often serves as a source of anxiety and complacency for its inheritors, thus making it hard for individuals to spend time in solitude, where they must be patient in the formulation of questions and in listening to responses.

Given the pace and competitiveness of the modern world, however, those without comparable material wealth can *also* neglect solitude in their pursuit of achievement. For many years, I was a reflection of this. Neither of my parents having attended university, and being the oldest of three boys raised by a single mother, I developed in secondary school a considerable work ethic that intensified throughout my undergraduate studies. It became my goal to win the Rhodes Scholarship, and so predictably I worked very hard to achieve this. Thankfully, this goal never came to be. I would interview as a finalist, though it is clear, in hindsight, that I was definitely not what they were looking for![1] (In hindsight, I'm afraid of what this would have led to had I won.)

My story is not unique. Many individuals not from privileged backgrounds lose themselves at points, if not entirely, in the pursuit of achievement. They become fixated on a lofty goal, tunneling on this at the expense of the ability to step back and think about what *actually* drives them, what they care about and why they hold particular views. They neglect to spend time in solitude and in so doing close themselves off from genuine self-criticism. In my case, I was fortunate to have a mother, several professors and a particular close friend who collectively provided me with honest and at times painful feedback about negative qualities that risked causing some personal harm in the future. Running a business for several years has likewise been formative in providing a reality check on life, most small business owners learning pretty quickly that good intentions do not always translate into productive outcomes. These sorts of "hard knocks" are valuable in that they help teach "street smarts."

These examples hopefully provide us with greater clarity in addressing the first part of the question about access, which focuses on a person's capacity in solitude to formulate questions and listen to responses effectively (that is, with honesty, patience and seriousness). It seems that the answer to this question is *no*—that material advantages do not necessarily enrich solitude. In fact, they sometimes do the opposite.

A reason for this, I believe, lies in how we consider the social dimension of solitude. Both material wealth and the lack of material wealth can contribute to false identity and so muddy the thinking that occurs in solitude. What matters instead is that particular kinds of influences exist *around* a person, and here I refer to individuals who are serious, truthful and thoughtful in their conversations with us. The greatest of friends are those who care about others such that they sometimes help reveal uncomfortable aspects of our lives. When delivered with fairness, love and care for the other person, these jolts provide much-needed perspective in the framing of our lives.

When this honesty exists, it is then possible to take more complete advantage of our time in solitude. It is in this sense that material advantages do not really enrich solitude. What matters instead is *how* a person uses social experience in the formulation of questions and the subsequent listening that takes place. The materials that a person uses as part of the search in solitude are informed by the unique circumstances of an individual life, but they can only be taken advantage of when it is a *person's genuine aim* to more clearly and seriously understand their true identity. That is, individuals must take responsibility for the practice of solitude.

The first half of the question now addressed, what are we to say about individuals' access *to* solitude? To start, when discussing access to solitude, what I mean is that individuals are able to choose to spend time in solitude. In considering the work of Mullainathan and Shafir, I worry that individuals attempting to escape from the scarcity trap will face considerable loneliness. Millennials who do not have material advantages, and who are either unemployed or underemployed, are here the objects of my focus. If an individual is forced to work in multiple jobs in order to make ends meet, or if job searches consume the bulk of one's attention due to the transition from one short-term contract to another, then we should consider whether it even makes sense to advocate for the practice of solitude. In this setting, solitude might be a cost, for it does not contribute to finding better employment and thus only perpetuates a low standard of living.

My sense is that solitude is still important, if not vital, for individuals caught in these situations. Solitude, when an active choice on the part of the person, provides opportunities to ask good questions, which can help a person climb out of scarcity traps. A blessing in disguise, here, might even be that necessity *sharpens the mind*. That said, without a sufficiently robust public support system, covering individuals' basic needs such as health, education and safety, solitude can only help so much. It is necessary, in order make the most of solitude, that one believes that one's efforts *matter*, even if only incrementally as part of a larger whole.

Though scarcity can be a source of anxiety and uncertainty—levying a "bandwidth tax," as Mullainathan and Shafir write—it sometimes provides chances for individuals to search more deeply within themselves.

Necessity can help individuals make sense of their lives in a way that is much less achievable when material resources are already at their disposal, for necessity provides a sense of urgency in making good decisions. Although material resources provide individuals with considerable time and space for contemplation—since those with safety nets beneath them can more easily take time off from their commitments—these same resources can also contribute to complacency in the personal search. Having a myriad of options seemingly at our fingertips reduces pressure to make decisions, and with this, the importance of thinking hard about what comes next. Simply put, individuals in these situations can take their sweet time. As a result, honesty becomes much less important in self-examination, for there are fewer consequences associated with living under a false identity. One can revert to a safety net whenever a given path doesn't pan out.

In summary, whereas it might be possible for millennials with comparatively greater material resources to engage in solitude, these very advantages can serve as barriers to self-reflection. The opportunities of time and space that material security provides lessen the perceived need for the practice of solitude. Conversely, while I acknowledge that it is more difficult for individuals with few material resources at their disposal to practice solitude, scarcity can spur a special kind of solitude in which considerable honest self-confrontation, conducted out of necessity, occurs. Put differently, material "disadvantage" can be channeled such that it contributes to a spiritual enrichment of self. This requires considerable will and perseverance.

This leads us to very briefly consider solitude as a *political* concept. My fear in public dialogue about solitude—assuming that this topic continues to garner more public attention in the coming years, as I sense it will—is that it will be used as a way to shift responsibility for material scarcity onto the individual. Entrepreneurship has suffered from this kind of thinking. Individuals in challenging socioeconomic circumstances are often told that, really, what they need to do is start companies in order to improve their situations.

Research suggests, however, that a significant portion of entrepreneurship is undertaken by those *already* in possession of considerable material resources, a fact that we encountered in Part I. Though I suggest that solitude can serve as a means to considerable self-understanding for those in difficult circumstances, necessity sharpening focus, honesty and intensity, this does not mean that individuals in these kinds of circumstances should be left to fend for themselves.

The work of Mullainathan and Sharif is indicative of how individuals behave en masse: generally, those in situations of scarcity tunnel on immediate needs, which takes time and energy away from thinking about long-term questions in much depth. It is in this sense that many individuals are at a disadvantage, and where effective public policy is needed. I have previously remarked that it is not my aim in this book to prescribe solutions for solitude—and so I similarly do not wish to venture into the question of specific public policy—but it is nevertheless important that we consider in our public dialogue about solitude the *potential* for this to become politicized as has been the case with some advocacy for entrepreneurship. Ultimately, solitude is a deeply personal activity, one that demands individual responsibility, but this does not mean that a public emphasis on solitude should make the individual entirely responsible for their personal struggles.

## COMMUNITY

A further criticism of solitude is that it weakens community, specifically at a time when communities are disintegrating. The work of Robert Putman, discussed earlier, is well known on this front. In addition to this, Angie Thurston and Casper ter Kuile offer a lens into millennials' community participation (or lack thereof) in their report *How We Gather*, in which they provide case studies of progressive faith-based initiatives in the United States. They write that "millennials are less religiously affiliated than ever before. According to the 2012 Pew Research Center report "'Nones' on the Rise," nearly one in three do not belong to a faith community and of those, only 10% are looking for one."[2] The authors later note that "the lack of deep community is indeed keenly felt," but that "in some cases, they [millennials] are creating what they don't find."[3]

The lack of deep community is indeed keenly felt, as the above writers show. In Part II, we examined the Global Shapers Community, which is considered by many of its members to be a progressive twenty-first-century community (one in which members interact from all parts of the world—Mumbai, Vladivostok, Halifax, Birmingham, etc.). However, in this and other modern communities, the relations between members are often rather transactional. One might say cosmopolitan. Membership churns rapidly as most individuals only participate for two or three years (if that) before moving on to other things. The most committed Global Shapers are exceptions—to their credit, some engage over many years. But in general, the community is rather individualistic: I've not yet been convinced that most members are not in it mainly for the brand value.

Elsewhere, many faith-based institutions struggle to attract those in their twenties and thirties, young people viewing these institutions as being too authoritative, traditional and static for their liking. I frequently hear religiously affiliated young people say that they are religious only in a cultural sense, or their religious affiliation valuable to them insofar as it helps them articulate *their* personal values. Put differently, one might say that millennials do not like to acknowledge external sources of wisdom, this recognition appearing to be antithetical to self-actualization. Hence, communities that involve commitments, in which tradition and authority play important roles, are to be avoided. Transactional communities are preferable in the modern world.

But the journey that takes place without regard to traditions leads, as I have indicated in Part I, to anxiety, these journeys often rather directionless. As the philosopher Charles Taylor writes, these journeys involve the consideration of many *intermediary* questions, though without necessarily leading to distinguishable overarching questions. Consequently, individuals push forward in their journeys, consistently acquiring new experiences but without the capacity to frame these within a coherent framework. Faith-based communities help resolve this. Although looked unfavorably upon today, they serve as potential corrections to the uncertainty and anxiety so prevalent in the modern world. These provide individuals with robust external sources of wisdom and guidance to which they can turn as they reflect on their inner selves.

Ultimately, we are in need of communities that offer individuals a sense of their history. That is, that provide continuity between the present and the past— that are enduring and that articulate a set of ends that can help individuals live "wisely, agreeably, and well," as Keynes writes. Faith-based communities are conducive to solitude in that they contribute to the awareness of our limitedness. They help ensure that individuals engage in dialogue about worthwhile goods: what kinds of things are worth valuing and why. These interactions can be enriching, but they can also be unpleasant, taking place with those with whom we differ in many ways *despite* holding certain beliefs and interests in common. This provides individuals with a greater sense of their strengths and flaws, and thus serves as a basis from which solitude can meaningfully take place.

It is in being truthful with ourselves that we can recognize flaws in our character, that there are behaviors that we should perhaps change. And it is in solitude that we are able to consider more fully previous conversations with colleagues, reflecting on which, of the things that we have heard, we agree or disagree with. Solitude, then—through the opportunity that it provides to better understand who we are as *individuals*—helps lay the groundwork for, and enriches, community. It is merely one factor in fostering community, and it does so only subtly, but it is nevertheless an important one.

As it currently stands, millennials, shaped by modern life, tend to believe that growth involves the relentless acquisition of experience, these experiences helping articulate values that exist within ourselves. But while it is understandable why a person might think this way, this mentality creates more anxiety than it does meaning. New forms of community are needed. The authors of *How We Gather* remark that "family, in all its forms, can be where we find our richest experience of love and belonging."[4] Following on this, they consider two questions: "What can these organizations learn about deep community from the institution of family? And how might strengthening communities actually strengthen families along the way?"[5]

Families provide love, care and affection, and in so doing can inspire individuals to be their best selves, living as they *are* as human beings. They are the strongest of commitments. They provide an individual with grounding, affection, authenticity and honesty, but because of these very qualities can also be the source of temporary hurt. But these ingredients are paramount in modern life, for they provide the existential security needed to practice solitude, secure with ourselves and with our questions and responses, without feeling the need to perform and share results.

## EDUCATION

A third concern pertains to modern education. Specifically, the aims and structure of university education (I shall here focus on universities) educate individuals *out of* spending time with themselves. Because of this, it becomes difficult for individuals to practice solitude as they age, having not developed an appreciation for aloneness during a particularly formative part of life.

Universities, pulled in many directions, cite a smorgasbord of activities of which they are a part, some more important than others: opening students' minds to the world; connecting students to communities; commercializing research; serving as economic engines; producing employable graduates; helping students expand their networks; educating students in a particular field or set of fields. It would be quite a stretch to say that universities now seek to inform their students in particular traditions. The plurality of activities that currently marks university education ensures that very little overlap in beliefs and values occurs between students from different departments or faculties within a given university. If there is any single idea that brings students together, it is that they need to find jobs, and that university degrees are probably not very helpful in achieving this (unless of course one is an engineer or a doctor).

One might think that universities provide time and space for aloneness and in turn solitude, but that is certainly not reflective of the lives that faculty and students now lead. The former are tasked with an increasing number of responsibilities (not only must they undertake teaching and research; it is now important that they demonstrate "impact" in their work). The latter feel that they must do more in order to market themselves to the workforce. As is the case with human beings, universities do not spend nearly enough time in their own purposeful self-reflection, confronting themselves by asking what they are really for. The question "Why?" is rarely sincerely posed. Indeed, there is strikingly little public dialogue pertaining to what universities are for.

While at the University of Alberta, I was consistently dismayed by the lack of meaningful public dialogue about where the university was headed and what it believed to be of most significance in undergraduate education. Most of the worthwhile conversations on this topic took place among professors behind closed doors, and therefore were of little value to the public. There was, I think, a thirst on campus for public dialogue, but few individuals were courageous enough to actually lead these conversations.

Academics, contrary to the spirit in which scholarship should be undertaken (mutual exploration in the pursuit of truth), often undermine each other as they hold tightly to their respective territories. Faculty are pressured to do more and more, but they are not usually productive contributors to public dialogue. Adding to this, university protest movements, now taking place across the United States, Canada and Europe regarding "safe spaces" for discussion, certainly do not further the pursuit of truth in higher education.

Several reforms, however, could simultaneously help universities be themselves, and in so doing enrich students' individual relationships with solitude. The first of these would be to drop all language about competitiveness, prosperity and economic contribution to society from university speeches, marketing material and other forms of communication. This would require political will on the part of university leadership, not to mention on the part of government.

In line with the shift in language, universities would also remove themselves from university rankings, these only institutionalizing the needless focus on competitiveness. These rankings are largely fluff, anyway, with many universities' positions fluctuating drastically from one year to the next as ranking methodologies change. If universities were to say decisively that they do not really care about economic prosperity and that it is not their role to think about whether their students graduate "workforce ready," then I do not think that governments or employers would put up much of a fight—each of these also lacking clarity as to what they stand for.

Second, universities would no longer refer to students as "customers," and they would attempt to narrow the courses from which students can choose. Every student would need to take several courses in philosophy, history, literature and related subjects within the liberal arts and participation in these courses would be taken seriously. In other words, these courses would not be seen as courses that students must take due to degree requirements, but rather, courses that are fundamental in any degree program. Students in this environment would then worry less about selecting courses that provide them with skills conducive to finding a job. The course selection would largely be done for them, the university demonstrating conviction as to the courses that it believes matter.

Professors in these courses would enrich students' understanding of what it means to be human. Moreover, universities would structure degree programs such that students take *fewer* courses. This is, I think, one of the most refreshing elements of the British tutorial system. Participating in only several courses at any one time, many consisting of small seminars, students actually have time to think about and discuss what they learn. Conversely, this is one of the real disadvantages, as I see it, in much of North American higher education, the volume of coursework and assessment in degree programs being such that students find it difficult to spend time actually thinking about what they learn.

Finally, universities would provide students with more time *off*. Again, there is much to learn from the British system. The academic year usually involves three eight-week terms, these punctuated by six-week breaks. A "long vacation" then takes place over the summer. This approach is conducive to solitude, students provided with the time and space to be alone and reflect on what they have just learned during the term. It is clear, perhaps, that my suggestions are largely applicable to North American culture, there generally being less time provided to students for vacation.

While the greater amount of time off does not necessarily bring about solitude, it at least helps set conditions for this to take place. Ultimately, the solitude that I have described in Part III involves qualities such as patience, honesty and a sense of the private. It is the manner in which universities *talk about themselves* that I see as being the most important factor in helping students engage in solitude. If universities regard themselves as economic engines, then no amount of academic reform will make much of a difference in their general disposition toward learning.

I have now addressed what I see as three of the major concerns that must be raised when advocating for solitude. The first of these pertains to access, considering questions such as "Who can access solitude?" and then "In what ways?" I argue that perceived material advantages can actually be unfavorable for individuals in understanding who they are, the increased comfort sometimes contributing to complacency. When individuals have a safety net beneath them, there is less urgency in spending time in solitude. A person can be lighthearted in decision-making, without facing too negative of repercussions should one decide poorly.

Of particular importance is the *manner* in which experience is framed. Individuals in situations of scarcity face barriers in their access to solitude; however, I suggest that these disadvantages can in some cases become advantages. I also recognize that it is possible for solitude to become politicized—as is the case with the promotion of entrepreneurship—and state that solitude should not be used as a way to shift too much responsibility onto individuals for the hardships that they might experience.

Additionally, I consider the view that solitude runs counter to community. In the writing of this book, friends and colleagues sometimes remarked that solitude takes individuals away from each other, precisely when communities are shriveling. The implication is that solitude is individualistic, the behavior of a recluse rather than of a bridge-builder. In response to this, I state that solitude and community are mutually reinforcing concepts. Particular kinds of communities (and here I mention faith-based communities, though communities needn't of course be limited to this) are enduring, informed by histories, traditions and practices that stand the test of time. These provide individuals with a sense of coherence in their lives, while simultaneously conveying a sense of human limitedness.

Finally, I identify several facets of modern university education that discourage individuals from thinking for themselves. Most important is the language that universities use when trying to make sense of what they do. This is a philosophical consideration: a shift in university language must precede structural reform if we are to enhance students' relationships with solitude. Specifically, universities must stop talking about their roles as economic engines. In addition to this, I highlight the British model's emphasis on dialogue and time *off* as being conducive to solitude.

The concerns addressed in this chapter are by no means exhaustive, though I believe they are three of the most formidable claims that can be made against solitude. My hope is that this chapter serves as a jumping-off point, from which more conversation about practical considerations pertaining to solitude can take place.

## NOTES

1   I was outright rejected, no interview, in my second application.
2   Angie Thurston, and Casper ter Kuile, *How We Gather*, 4. Available from: https://caspertk.files.wordpress.com/2015/04/how-we-gather.pdf.
3   Ibid.
4   Ibid., 18.
5   Ibid.

# CONCLUSION

The modern journey involves considerable exploration, but it is beset by anxiety—anxiety that one is not keeping pace, not doing or accomplishing enough, not living up to potential. In a world of affluence, individuals are constantly aware of the lives that they could lead, if only they wanted to. For all of the perceived benefits, a belief in limitless potential—the ability for individuals to change the world—produces frustration and disappointment. The more one does and accomplishes, the greater the imagined opportunities become. At the same time, the many pressures of modern life quiet the inner voice that asks, even if weakly, "How much is enough?"

What matters in modern life is that experiences are acquired and then articulated for public consumption. It is not enough that individuals participate in new activities, see new places or meet new people; these activities are to be curated and carefully presented to others. As Turkle notes, the performance of identity becomes identity itself. Specifically, these performances require that individuals be adaptable, for it is adaptability that provides a semblance of continuity in a world that is believed to be evolving more rapidly than ever, one in which demands for skills are shifting and where the most enduring of traditions are contested. The point is not to settle, for this represents a slowing down, an admission that one cannot keep up with the demands of modern life—an abandonment of ambition.

When the world is replete with uncertainty, knowledge becomes fragile and relationships are less likely to endure. Adaptability is therefore believed to be critical: it is on the surface the most sensible guidance that universities can provide to students and the most reasonable of strategies for progression in the workforce. Given our culture of performance, this facilitated in large part through our online lives, it is better to go with the flow than to stop and critically examine what performance really entails. To reflect in this way would be considered too serious. Modern commitments are, after all, light.

For individuals coming of age, what matters is that one discovers oneself, pushing through personal limits in the journey for meaning and the articulation of personal values. But the very hyperconnectedness, competitiveness and speed with which the search takes place draws individuals away from themselves. Performance informs identity, but it does not follow that identity is authentic. Cheap security, as Williams says, is more likely. The millennial journey is often replete with self-deception, uncertainty and a lingering sense that something important—but that is difficult to put a finger on—is lacking. One knows that values and knowledge are important, but wonders why these things alone are not helpful in answering fundamental questions: in particular, who we are as reflective *individuals* embedded in social structures.

I argue in this book that for millennials, few activities are more important than solitude—but not for the reasons typically imagined. Differentiating solitude from aloneness and loneliness, I argue that solitude must take place in physical aloneness, but that it is more specifically a philosophical search in one's aloneness. It is a search and clarification of questions pertaining to one's life, accompanied by a patient and honest listening to the responses. I worry, as a practitioner, having worked with and observed millennials across multiple countries over the last years, about the language nowadays used to describe what kinds of lives are worth leading. Wants, needs and desires prevail: in short, the individual comes prior to the social. This contributes to a millennial *malaise* (to borrow from the language of Charles Taylor).

I do not attempt to say in this book what millennials are, but rather to provide a particular interpretation of social, economic, cultural and educational conditions that I believe collectively shape how individuals, at a formative time in their lives, come to think and behave. My sense is that public discourse about what it means to live a good life is severely impoverished. Young people consume information, but without grounding in relation to wise persons and traditions that transcend the self, knowledge can only be tenuous.

I recognize that solitude is, in many people's eyes, antithetical to progress. To find time and space for oneself means that one is not active in a "doing" sense. Solitude is a search, and so it requires patience—particularly as one grows frustrated when expectations for fast answers in solitude are not met. I argue that solitude requires a sense of the private: the questions that one formulates and the responses that one receives in careful listening, are *not* to be shared, at least not in the short term.

Part of the beauty of solitude is that one can sit on things, making sense of them in one's own time. The practice of this kind of solitude is, as I see it, courageous when societal pressures encourage constant activity. Solitude requires that individuals do not begin their searches with particular expectations or outcomes in mind, and yet the immateriality of the process produces in the long term the most enriching of outcomes.

If we believe in the individual, then there are particular kinds of questions that we must be able to answer for ourselves: "What do *I* think about this?"; "What matters to *me*?"; "What kind of person do *I* want to become?" To be an individual is to be able to answer—or at the very least, seriously and continuously consider—these questions in relation to challenges that we individually encounter. I've written this book in large part because, when looking at many of my peers and the modern world more generally, I fear that individuals are pushed in the opposite direction. I too struggle with these questions and pressures.

Millennials, I think, are pushed to perform for others, but lose a sense of who they are, as individuals, in their constant striving to fulfill a nebulous sense of potential. This book serves as an attempt to articulate these and other challenges that a significant number of people nowadays face. More importantly, it hopefully encourages us to cultivate relationships with ourselves—aware of our limitations and strengths alike. The world is changing quickly and the problems that young people are set to inherit are formidable. But action is most powerful when informed through patience and honesty in critical self-examination.

# BIBLIOGRAPHY

Adams, Susan. "The 10 Skills Employers Most Want in 20-Something Employees." *Forbes*, October 11, 2013.

Advisory Council on Economic Growth. "Building a Highly Skilled and Resilient Canadian Workforce Through the FutureSkills Lab." 2017.

Bandura, Albert. "The Psychology of Chance Encounters and Life Paths." *American Psychologist* 37, no. 7 (1982): 749.

Bandura, Albert, and Jourden Forest. "Self-Regulatory Mechanisms Governing the Impact of Social Comparison on Complex Decision Making." *Journal of Personality and Social Psychology* 60, no. 6 (1991): 943–50.

Barnett, Ronald. "Learning for an Unknown Future." *Higher Education Research & Development* 23, no. 3 (2004): 67.

Barr, Caelainn, and Malik Shiv. "Revealed: The 30-Year Economic Betrayal Dragging Down Generation Y's Income." *The Guardian*, March 7, 2016.

Bell. "Let's Talk," *Our Initiatives*. 2018. Available from: https://letstalk.bell.ca/en/our-initiatives/.

Brooker, Nathan. "London Housing: Too Hot for Young Buyers." *Financial Times*, April 27, 2017.

Brooks, David. *The Road to Character*. New York: Random House, 2015.

Carmichael, Sarah Green. "Millennials Are Actually Workaholics According to Research." *Harvard Business Review*, August 17, 2016.

Carney, Mark. "Inclusive Capitalism: Creating a Sense of the Systemic." Bank of England, May 27, 2014. Available from: http://www.fsb.org/wp-content/uploads/Carney-Inclusive-Capitalism-Creating-a-sense-of-the-systemic.pdf.

Clarke, Thurston. *The Last Campaign*. New York: Henry Holt, 2008.

Clifford, Matt. "Technology Entrepreneurship and the Disruption of Ambition." *Medium*, January 24, 2017.

Columbia University Center for Career Education. *Leadership Development & Rotational Programs*. 2018. Available from: https://www.careereducation.columbia.edu/resources/leadership-development-rotational-programs.

Crane, Brent. "The Virtues of Isolation." *Atlantic*, March 30, 2017.

Crockett, Zachary. "Millennials Have Very Little Confidence in Most Major Institutions." *Vox*, September 28, 2016.

Department for Business Innovation & Skills; Department of Education. *Post-16 Skills Plan*, July 2016.

Dewey, John. *The Public and Its Problems*. Athens: Swallow Press & Ohio University Press, 1954.

Elias, John, and Sharan Merriam. *Philosophical Foundations of Adult Education*. Malabar: Krieger Publishing, 2005.

Ferguson, Brad. "Don't Apologize for Your Liberal Arts Degree." *Globe and Mail*, March 27, 2014.

Gladwell, Malcolm. "The Talent Myth." *New Yorker*, July 22, 2002.

Global Shapers Community. *Introducing the Global Shapers Community*. "Building a Movement." 2018. Available from: https://www.globalshapers.org/story.

Groth, Aimee. "Entrepreneurs Don't Have a Special Gene for Risk—They Come from Families with Money." *Quartz*, July 17, 2015.

Hamilton, Kirk-Anthony. "Who Are the Global Shapers?" *Huff Post*, September 3, 2015.

Howard, Caroline. "Meet the 2017 Class of 30 under 30." *Forbes*, January 3, 2017.

Howard, Caroline, and Sportelli, Natalie. "Presenting the 2018: 30 Under 30." *Forbes*, 2018. Available from: https://www.forbes.com/30-under-30/2018/#c834b1a1aaf4.

Kalb, Bess. "A Selection of the 30 Most Disappointing Under 30." *New Yorker*, January 5, 2017.

Keegan, Marina. "Even Artichokes Have Doubts." *Yale Daily News*, September 30, 2011.

Khinda, Navneet, and Dongwoo Kim. "Selfishness Defines Gen Y Entrepreneurs." *Globe and Mail*, March 28, 2014.

Laing, Olivia. *The Lonely City: Adventures in the Art of Being Alone*. Edinburgh: Canongate, 2016.

Manyika, James, Susan Lund, Jacques Bughin, Kelsey Robinson, Jan Mischke, and Deepa Mahajan. "Independent Work: Choice, Necessity, and the Gig Economy." *McKinsey Global Institute*, October 2016.

Marano, Hara Estroff. "What Is Solitude?" *Psychology Today*, July 1, 2003.

Marche, Stephen. "Is Facebook Making Us Lonely?" *Atlantic*, April 3, 2012.

Mullainathan, Sendhil, and Eldar Shafir. *Scarcity: The True Cost of Not Having Enough*. New York: Times Books, 2013.

Nahar, Jasmin. "21 Tweets for Millennials Who Are Just Tired of Bullshit." *BuzzFeed*, May 16, 2017.

Oakeshott, Michael. *Rationalism in Politics and Other Essays*. Indianapolis: Liberty Fund, 1991.

Phillips, Adam. *Missing Out: In Praise of the Unlived Life*. London: Hamish Hamilton, 2012.

Poverty and Employment Precarity in Southern Ontario. "The Precarity Penalty: The Impact of Employment Precarity on Individuals, Households and Communitie— and What To Do About It." May 2015.

Pryor, Lisa. "Doctors Are Human Too." *New York Times*, April 21, 2017.

Reed, Mariel. "What Is the World Economic Forum Global Shapers Community, Really?" *Medium*, July 30, 2017.

Rohrer, Finlo. "The Slow Death of Purposeless Walking." *BBC News Magazine*, May 1, 2014.

Roksa, Josipa, and Richard Arum. *Academically Adrift: Limited Learning on College Campuses*. Chicago: University of Chicago Press, 2011.

Royal Society for Public Health. *#StatusofMind*. 2017.

Rutter, Tamsin. "How to Join the Civil Service Fast Stream." *The Guardian*, September 1, 2015.

Sandel, Michael. *What Money Can't Buy: The Moral Limits of Markets*. New York: Farrar, Straus and Giroux, 2012.

Schaeper, Thomas, and Kathleen Schaeper. *Rhodes Scholars, Oxford, and the Creation of an American Elite*. New York: Berghahn Books, 2010.

Schwab, Klaus. "The Fourth Industrial Revolution: What It Means, How to Respond." *World Economic Forum*, January 14, 2016. Sennett, Richard. *The Craftsman*. London: Penguin Books, 2008.

Shulte, Brigid. "Time in the Bank: A Stanford Plan to Save Doctors from Burnout." *Washington Post*, August 20, 2015.

Simon, Ruth, and Caelainn Barr. "Endangered Species: Young U.S. Entrepreneurs." *Wall Street Journal*, January 2, 2015.

Skidelsky, Robert. *Keynes: The Return of the Master*. London: Penguin Books, 2009.

Spicer, André, and Carl Cederström. *The Wellness Syndrome*. Cambridge: Polity, 2015.

Sullivan, Andrew. "I Used to Be a Human Being." *New York Magazine*, September 18, 2016.

Tawney, Richard Henry. *The Acquisitive Society*. London: G. Bell and Sons, 1921.

Taylor, Charles. *Sources of the Self: The Making of Modern Identity*. Cambridge: Cambridge University Press, 1989.

TD Bank Group. *The Impact of Income Volatility on Canadians: A Public Opinion Survey Conducted on Behalf of TD Bank Group*. April 23, 2017.

Thurston, Angie, and Casper ter Kuile. "How We Gather." 2015. Available from: https://caspertk.files.wordpress.com/2015/04/how-we-gather.pdf.

Todd, Benjamin, "Want to Do Good? Here's How to Choose an Area to Focus on?" 80,000 Hours, March 2017.

Turkle, Sherry. *Alone Together*. New York: Basic Books, 2011.

Weber, Max. *The Protestant Ethic and the Spirit of Capitalism*. London: George Allen & Unwin, 1930.

Whitehead, Alfred North. *The Aims of Education and Other Essays*. London: Williams & Northgate, 1932.

Williams, Rowan. *Open to Judgement: Sermons and Addresses*. London: Darton, Longman and Todd, 1994.

Yu, Serena, Tanya Bretherton, Johanna Schutz, and John Buchanan. Working Paper. "Understanding the Nature of Vocations Today: Exploring Labour Market Pathways." Workplace Research Centre University of Sydney, October 22, 2012.

# INDEX

147

Lightning Source UK Ltd.
Milton Keynes UK
UKHW040811280319
340051UK00006B/310/P